THE FLEXIFOIL BOOK OF
POWER KITING

Navigator Guides Ltd
The Old Post Office, Swanton Novers
Melton Constable, Norfolk NR24 2AJ
info@navigatorguides.com
www.navigatorguides.com

Copyright © Navigator Guides Ltd 2002, 2003, 2007
ISBN 9781903872161

Acknowledgements

Navigator Guides would like to thank all those at Flexifoil International for the enormous contribution they have made to the publishing of this book, but a special mention to Jeremy Pilkington for the introduction to Jeremy Boyce, an inspired choice of writer, to all at SCW especially Claire Hawkes for the design, and to Andrew Jones and Mike Shaw for their technical advice and input. Likewise, Nick Goodyear for the brilliant cover design, Paul Thody from Air Born Kites, Matt Taggart from Ozone Kites and J from ATB Mag. for special technical advice. To all you mad people out there who keep making it all happen. And finally to Jeremy Boyce for all his hard work and constant enthusiasm for the project.

Text Design: SCW www.scwuk.com
Cover Design: Nick Goodyear

Illustrations by Liz Johnson
Contributors: Andrew Jones and Mike Shaw
Photographers: Alan Pritchard, Andrew Jones, Carol Kohen, Christian Black, Dan Eaton, Jono Knight, John Carter, Ray Merry, Ronny Kiaulehn and Jane Rankin
Proofreading: Susannah Wight

Printed in China by 1010 Printing International Ltd

THE FLEXIFOIL BOOK OF
POWER KITING

JEREMY BOYCE

CONTENTS

Jason in action

I've tried most extreme sports at one time or another, and loved each one for the incredible buzz they had to offer, but I had no idea that powerkiting would end up taking over my life as it has. Power kites really have got something for everyone whatever their level.

Flexifoil International is a 100% kite power organisation. They invented the sport and they've been inventing, developing and promoting power kites of all types for nearly 30 years. I first got involved with Flexi in 1994, and since then I've flown and tested every Flexifoil power kite to its absolute limits. Flexifoil took a gamble, supporting and sponsoring me when I was relatively unknown in competition racing on kite buggies. With their support I went on to become UK, European & World Kite Buggy Champion.

By 1996 I'd achieved everything I wanted or could in kite buggies and had loads of fun along the way. But kiteboarding had bitten me bad and I really believed it would be the 'next big thing'…

At this stage Flexifoil's only water kite was the Blade, a kite that was in its infancy, a conventional ram air traction kite designed primarily for high-end land-based power But by this time it was clear that kiteboarding was really taking off and that the market for 'water' kites was shifting in a new direction, away from Flexifoil's traditional strengths in ram air kites. Flexifoil joined in the charge towards kites that were fully water re-launchable and after many ideas, prototypes and test sessions, the Storm inflatable kite was to be the next breakthrough and, in keeping with Flexifoil tradition, a great success. The Storm 2 and 3 were perfect next step developments, consolidating Flexifoil's position in the new market, followed by the superb Strike, Fusion, Ion and Atom. These kites have established the company as a serious competitor in the potentially huge world kiteboarding market.

It's more than fifteen years since I first got involved in power kites and it's fantastic to see that kiteboarding is now the fastest growing water sport in the world. A factor that is helping powerkiting as a whole worldwide: there's never been more interest in kite power than now. When you think about the potential crossovers from so many other sports like surfing, windsurfing, sailing, snowboarding, skiing, water skiing, paragliding, skateboarding, mountain boarding etc. the future for powerkiting looks like my own powerkite style – no-limits. And when you've believed in this sport for as long as I have, it's fantastic to see the whole thing booming. I'm really excited to see what the future has in store, power kite ships, power kites in space… Who knows ?

Go well, Fly safe, Have fun

Jason Furness, Flexifoil Kiteboarder Team Manager, Power Kite Fanatic
May 2007

HISTORY

4

INTRODUCTION

You may find this hard to believe, but there was a time – not that long ago – when there were no such things as mobile phones and texting, no PC in every house, no internet, no cybercafés, no such thing as CDs, MP3s or iPods, no satellite TV or CCTV, no such things as SUVs or Quad Bikes, no out-of-town superstores or Multiplex cinemas. Worse still, there were literally no such things as power kites either. How things have changed. Yes, we've all benefited a tiny bit from some of those technological advances, although let's be fair, none of them have actually been made without somebody somewhere crying 'foul'. But the world is unquestionably a richer place for the invention of power kites, back in the 1970s, and subsequent harnessing of them to all manner of boards, karts and other movable contraptions. The kitebuggy was first to make an impact, but more people nowadays will be familiar with the power kite sport that has brought the whole activity to the attention of the masses: kiteboarding. Kiteboarding and its spin-offs (including kite landboarding and snowkiting) have introduced many thousands of newcomers to the wonderful, no-limits world of power kiting, turning it into a global extreme sport on the verge of break-

◀ The original : a big stack of Flexifoil Stacker 6 kites
▶ Ray Merry and Andrew Jones

ing through into the big league. Like many such activities, one company and its innovative product kicked the whole thing off…

The first modern power kite, Flexifoil's 'Stacker 6', was conceived, designed and built in Britain almost 30 years ago – by two highly motivated people working from home – a true 'garden shed' beginning to what has now become a worldwide brand and which has spawned an entire industry. In many ways, the most surprising thing is that it's taken so long for their outstanding invention to grab the popularity it has, triggering so many spin-off activities (from simply flying the kites) along the way.

As with any great invention it's arguable that someone else would have thought of it if Flexifoil hadn't, but the point is, they did. And it's certainly true that there are now dozens of designers and manufacturers of highly competitive traction kites fuelling a rapidly growing industry, such is the current world wide interest in kite powered possibilities. You could say that Flexifoil have made possible the whole traction scene as we know it today.

How it all began

To get the full picture you have to make your way back through the mists of time to the mid 70s, back to a time when there were no stunt (i.e. two string, steerable) kites to be bought of any description. Then, madcap British inventor Peter Powell came up with his eponymous diamond shaped, long tailed stunter, a kite form much imitated since by manufacturers all over the world.

Around the same time, also in Britain, two design students – Andrew Jones and Ray Merry – were experimenting with a series of large format wind sculptures. They had built a series of sky tubes of increasingly scary dimensions (although they lacked a serious lifting device – such as a kite - for them, resorting to long poles and buildings to get them off the ground) before embarking on their ultimate project, an inflatable air-foil wing sculpture that could be tethered as a piece of temporary, movable, public art. They even mocked up photographs of the Grand Canyon, with their creation superimposed, showing clearly, even at this early stage, the instantly recognisable profile of the Flexifoil power kite wing. Although they started experimenting with wind devices as early as 1972, it wasn't until the late 70s, after a lengthy series of wind tunnel tests, that the first 'Flexifoils' appeared, made from polythene with an externally fitted cane leading-edge rod, but in essence the same kite that is still manufactured today as the top selling Stacker 6.

Whatever next?

The kites were an 'instant' success, in the limited terms of reference the kite industry offered at that time. They had difficulty keeping up with demand at first and expanded their operation by 50% by taking on experienced seamstress and kite legend in her own right, Jilly Pelham, to sew the kites — now made from ripstop nylon. The business grew quickly but despite (perhaps because of ?) this, Flexifoil themselves had to endure some setbacks and financial difficulties before passing into the hands of the Dutch van Dort family as part of their business portfolio, giving the company the stability that has allowed their subsequent advance to be almost relentless.

The concept of using kites for traction gradually began to export itself around the world, establishing links with other wind power freaks elsewhere. Among these was New Zealander, Peter Lynn. Where Jones and Merry had toyed with the idea of some kind of kart and even a boat towed by kites (Jacob's Ladder), Lynn advanced the concept several giant strides when, in the mid 80s, he began appearing at kite festivals on a custom designed and built steel-framed kite buggy. His three-wheel design (two rear wheels and a single front steering wheel operated by the feet, leaving hands free to control the kite/s) established a model that has not been challenged since. A Flexifoil kite buggy 2006 style retains that essential format, even if the detailing and fittings have evolved several leaps, as you would expect.

Kite buggying was born and taken up with enthusiasm by an informed and well-off minority in many countries. Not selling in significant numbers yet, buggy prices were very high because manufacturing volumes were very low. Also, kite buggying looked interesting but the type of kites to power the buggies available at that time didn't

◀ From radical power kiting on a kite buggy...

offer enough control or easy accessibility to the sport. Not that buggy drivers cared, they were happy to use what was there. Lynn produced a range of power kites of his own, the Peel series, then designed a production buggy for Flexifoil. All very friendly, even in business.

Also in the mid 80s Ray Merry left Flexifoil and Europe for America to set up Cobra Kites, a design and manufacturing company in its own right but also providing a distribution for Flexifoil kites in America. As the gospel spread, power kiting was slowly growing in popularity but lacked that something that would give it a quantum leap in terms of mass appeal. That process started at the beginning of the 90s when two significant steps forward were made that would 'revolutionise' the power kite world, both in America. It's hard to say which made the more significant contribution ultimately.

The first, however, shows a remarkable pioneering spirit and awareness of a possible commercial application that took another decade to come to fruition. The man who first took kites onto the water in a meaningful, not to mention successful, way was in the process of developing the equipment to do so. American Cory Roeseler saw the possibility and developed a rig, the 'Kiteski', that was an early forerunner of what we recognise today as kiteboarding. His single or double water skis combined with a huge, half-moon,

▶ ...to pure fun recreational flying, Flexifoil has something for everyone

rigid-framed, two-lined steerable kite, flown from a control bar fitted with motorised line winders, was eerily close to the arched kite shape and (twin-tip) board that have become such big business today. The fact that he'd already perfected his water starts and getting upwind in time to be demo-ing his rig in 1992–93, five full years before the sport even began to happen, shows how ahead of his time Roeseler was.

Second came the development of new control systems for kites which made buggying a far more viable possibility and later opened the door to numerous other kite- powered activities, enabling them to flourish to a much greater degree than might otherwise have been the case. The four control lines concept was devised at the end of the 80s by Revolution Enterprises, a San Diego based company run by the enigmatic Hadziki family, also specialising in the manufacture of high-quality carbon fibre rods for golf clubs, arrow shafts and, yes, kites. Their 'Revolution' four line framed kite and 'total control' slogan made their impact on power kite design when first Robert Graham's Quadrifoil company, then Ray Merry's new venture, Cobra Kites, released their Quadrifoil and Skytiger kites respectively, power kites which used Revolution's four line total control idea.

The realisation of Lynn-inspired production buggies and the advent of four line

▲ Jacob's Ladder: Flexifoil's first attempt to take power kites onto the water
◀ Water kiting today, the latest extreme sport, kiteboarding

power kites such as the Skytiger, which Flexifoil manufactured and distributed in Europe, provided the platform for the spectacular growth the industry has seen over the most recent decade. From the beaches where the buggies prospered it seemed a natural next step to take kites onto the water, but Roeseler's rig, interesting though it was, clearly wasn't practical or commercially viable enough. While all this was going on, over in France a pair of sailor designer cum adventurers, the Legaignoux brothers, had been working since the early 80s on a concept of their own, half kite, half sail, but, importantly, water re-launchable. They'd intended it to be compatible with a board for surfing but had never refined a working system. The closest they had come was an inflatable canoe to which the kite was anchored in order to drag it over the water. A third Frenchman joined the attack, Manu Bertin, a former world record holder at speed windsurf and hugely experienced waterman. His determination to make surfing with a kite, the Legaignoux's Wipika kite, work was largely responsible for kiteboarding starting when it did. And when he took his rig to Maui, the very epicentre for everything that surfs or boards in the world, for sure the cat was out of the bag. When opinion-forming movers and shakers such as windsurf legends Robby Naish and Pete Cabrinha jumped on board, quickly releasing their own ranges of boards and Wipika-inspired water re-launchable kites, it was clear that power kiting had taken on an altogether new dimension, one which has moved it relatively quickly up into the big league of extreme sports, a destination which, for a long time, it looked like it might never reach. Flexifoil have continued to be market leaders in air foil power kiting, but have also claimed a place in the fiercely competitive market for water re-launchables. The company now has a national and international rider team representing all the established kite traction sports. The commitment they showed in spotting and sponsoring young British rider Aaron Hadlow paid off handsomely when he won the PKRA World Championship in 2004 using Flexifoil's Storm and Strike kites. And the design team behind the latest Flexifoil kite successes now comprises fully informed aero-engineering and design boffins such as the Rebbeck brothers, Luke and Henry, with other specialists contributing control gear (bars and handles), safety features, landboard and buggy designs. Everything is quite literally much more measured; there's less and less room for leaving things to chance.

With increased sales and business size has come increased responsibility and risk, and it's true to say that Flexifoil has far more to lose now that what they started has progressed so far, not simply the garden shed but house, garage and car besides. But that's not a likely scenario as they're about as diversified as it's possible to be in power kiting,

▲ Power kiting into the record books, the Flexifoil 208 Stack at Le Touquet 1993

▶ Jason Furness cross-Channel kiteboarding 1999

9

their brand and products known around the world and emblematic of the entire sport.

Future perfect

The power kite market nowadays is a massive free-for-all. Not only have kites gone onto the water, they're increasingly pressed into service on the snow (boards or skis), ice, mountainboards, roller blades... Basically, anything you can do that moves, someone's going to try it faster, harder and up in the air on the end of a power kite, if they haven't already.

With all those specialisms have come ever more numerous manufacturers, keen for a piece of the action and a slice of the growing market that exists for power kiting in all its weird and wonderful forms. With them, technological input from other areas: sailmaking, windsurfing, paragliding... Competitiveness in the business has driven the rapid development of better and safer equipment, making the sport accessible in a way that it had always dreamed of being. From two blokes in a garden shed in Cambridgeshire to a worldwide industry with dozens of

manufacturers, thousands of players, millions of happy customers...

Interestingly many of those early pioneers are still there, heavily involved in the new aspects of kite power. Andrew Jones was, until mid 2005, still in position at Flexifoil and had seen the company become the single biggest pure power kite manufacturer in the world. He may no longer be working for Flexifoil but is still as involved in power kiting as ever as a design and development consultant. Peter Lynn is going stronger than ever down under with a full range of kites, boards and buggies; and Ray Merry's Cobra Kites are still preaching the traction gospel in America, as are the Legaignoux brothers with their Takoon company in France. Corey Roeseler too is still prominent in the scene, a pro kiteboard rider and equipment developer for the giant American sailmaking Gaastra company. The power kite scene has moved on a long way and swept a lot of people along with it. None of them knew where they were going when they started this thing and there's no telling where it'll go next. As power kite pioneer and Flexifoil co-designer Andrew Jones himself once said "It's just great to use the wind to go somewhere."

In every sense !

◀ Flexifoil team kiteboarders product testing in South Africa
▶ Fully kitted out for a fun day at the beach

BASICS

2

"I've jumped out of planes and everything but for me the buzz you can get from power kites stands on its own – something you have to have a lot of respect for, but with big rewards for sure."

JASON FURNESS, FLEXIFOIL DEMONSTRATOR AND INTERNATIONAL KITEBOARDER TEAM MANAGER

TO START WITH, TRY USING YOUR HEAD...

There almost couldn't be anything much more simple than flying a dual control line Flexifoil power kite. Think bike riding without the complication of pedalling to keep moving. To control the kite (bike) you move the handles or control bar push-me-pull-you style, pull right to turn right, pull left to turn left, hands parallel to go straight. All good kites come with basic instructions to tell you how to 'fly' them, but there are all kinds of dos and don'ts that you pick up with experience that help build your comprehension of how the wind and the kites work together to deliver the result you're looking for. That might mean pure recreational flying, it might mean serious traction sports, either way the result should be endless hours of fun and amusement. It may be simply for pleasure or it might all come together one day to save your own or someone else's life. No amount of instruction books and videos can make you into the perfect pilot because, ultimately, there's no substitute for getting out there and flying.

Once you get a Flexifoil power kite flying, you can completely control it and manoeuvre it exactly where you want it to go within its 'wind window'. The kite will want to move forwards almost all the time and it's up to your piloting skill to keep it moving without crashing into the ground or into any other kites, also to make sure that the flying lines never get so twisted by repeated turns in one direction that you lose all response from the kite. It might sound complicated but it actually requires less mental and physical agility than many everyday activities, such as booting up your new laptop and getting on the net.

◀ The Flexifoil Stacker 6, great for stacking...
▶ ...and single kite flying

Power kiting is an increasingly sophisticated sport and there's now a whole generation of manoeuvrable, traction kites out there with not just two, but four control lines, that are even more technically sophisticated, more controllable, kites which can, in the right circumstances, be manoeuvred even more precisely to deliver more and more consistent power and efficiency, yes, even boot up your laptop instead of having to ask your kids to do it for you… They have helped bring power kiting to where it is today, a sport with many layers of technicality and enjoyment, plus a general ease of use that explains much of its enormous present day popularity as an extreme sport and leisure pursuit. In short, a sport on the verge of greatness.

WHAT IS POWER KITING ALL ABOUT ?

"Power kiting is great, you can take it to whatever extreme you want, family day out or all the way. The first time I was shoved on a power kite I flew off down the beach and that was it, I was hooked. It was an

unbelievable feeling. We all know the power of the wind is immense, but to feel it in your hands is awesome!"

'Andreya Wharry, Flexifoil International team kiteboarder, Extreme Academy power kite instructor

Clearly we would in no way condone anyone flying out of control or attempting any 'serious' traction action before they're properly ready (not in print anyway), and under close supervision even then. Nevertheless, the short answer to the question 'what is power kiting all about?' is, the flying of large single or stacked (several kites linked together) manoeuvrable kites in such a way as to

◀ Top to bottom: Stacker 6, Proteam 8, Super 10
▶ Getting some radical air on a kite landboard

achieve traction, i.e. generally be dragged around, and often above, your chosen flying site by whatever means possible. This includes: skidding (being dragged along on your feet or back), jumping / getting airs, bodysurfing, landboarding, kitebuggying, kiteskating, kiteboating, kitewater-skiing, kiteskiing, kitesnowboarding, and last but by every means biggest, power kiting's current 'market leader', kiteboarding or kitesurfing.

The longer, and somewhat more considered, version of this (at least for insurance purposes) is that power kiting is all about learning how to use your kite and the elements, in this instance the wind and your physical location, in a safe and controlled manner so as to deliver the maximum of enjoyment with the minimum of risk. Modern power kiting equipment qualifies the sport as 'extreme'. That means extreme injuries, even fatalities, can occur (and indeed have occurred) if the proper respect and attention are not paid to what you are doing. That starts with yourself and applies equally to your equipment, the physical location and the weather conditions on the day. It means being certain that you know what you're doing and that you understand your limits and your equipment's limits and potential.

Whatever level you're doing this at, either for pure recreational pleasure now and then or because you want to be the big star rider on the kiteboarding pro tours, you must understand properly how your kite works before you start taking risks. Of course it's accepted that the attraction of any extreme sport is the risk factor and consequent adrenaline rush that comes with it. The trick is to make making the risk whether you succeed or not rather than whether you end up in hospital or not.

Successful power kiting means working out where your limits are and pushing them gradually further and further until you reach your desired level of skill and get the corresponding level of adrenaline 'buzz' which, for many, it's all about. Like many power kiters, you may find that, once hooked you can never get enough, always looking for more power and more danger (going faster, jumping higher etc.). That buzz comes at a price, one you should start paying straight away by reading the following safety advice rather than paying later in hospital or, worse still, in a costly damages or liability case.

SAFETY

Walk, don't run

In power kiting there can never be any question of who might be liable in the event of anything going horribly wrong, so I'll say this just once:

"SAFETY IS THE RESPONSIBILITY OF THE FLYER... !"

Just like most other extreme sports, for safety's sake you need to totally familiarise yourself with your equipment at the outset.

Learn how to properly control a kite of manageable size before you start risking life and limb on any of the large number of serious traction power kites on the market today. Once you've mastered the basics (which really shouldn't take that long) you'll be ready to get going with some of the big, adrenaline-inducing, buttock-clenching kites which extreme power kiting is all about. All the same, be ready to be shocked and surprised by just how much 'grunt' these kites can generate, and never, ever underestimate what can happen when you start playing around with the elements. Make sure you've fully mastered controlling every kite in your bag. What you take the time to learn today might well save a life tomorrow, your own or that of a colleague.

It's worth remembering that a kite is a sail, just like those on a yacht or windsurf rig, and it generates variable power / traction in relation to its size, position in the wind window and wind strength. The bigger the kite, the greater the power it can generate. The risk of personal injury through ignorance or simply a moment's carelessness is very real. As an opening piece of advice, let's say that if you are one of those people who falls hard and breaks easily then by all means try power kiting, but maybe extreme power kiting isn't for you. If, on the other hand, you know how to fall without hurting yourself, you don't bruise easily and you bounce rather than break, sinfully good times await…

You will need a reasonable level of fitness if you want to really get to grips with big kites. If you don't already have good fitness you will need to build that up, by flying smaller kites to begin with, before moving onwards and upwards, literally and metaphorically. The work out you get from the kites will help strengthen exactly the muscles you need, but torn muscles and tendons can easily happen, injuries that take time to mend and could keep you off the flying field for lengthy periods. Broken wrists, ankles and collar bones can too easily result from heavy landings on any surfaces (even water hurts when you crash into it on the end of a powered up water kite), or a steel-framed buggy hitting you after a wipe out. In any event you will find, after your first couple of sessions, that power kiting works on different muscles and in a different way than you are used to. Expect to feel pain in some unusual places as your body adjusts.

With the speed of technical innovation there has been in the sport recently, there are now lots of pieces of extra equipment and safety aids available to the modern power kiter, in many cases 'bolted onto' the kites, one of the many positive spin-offs of the emergence of kiteboarding, where it quickly became clear safety had to be a priority issue, in a way existing kite sports hadn't required up to then. Body harnesses, which you hook your kite control gear onto, are indispensa-

▲ Hard, flat sand as far as the eye can see, a perfect kite buggying spot

ble for kiteboarding, snowkiting, kitelandboarding and buggying, otherwise you couldn't cope with the huge pull of the kites for any length of time. Never, however, under any circumstances permanently attach yourself to the kite(s) with a fixed knot or other connection. No matter how good and experienced a kite flyer you are, the unexpected can always happen and you may need to separate yourself from the kite quickly. Quick releases, de-power systems, safety leashes, flotation jackets, crash helmets, knee and elbow pads, goggles etc. etc. are all part of the essential safety equipment nowadays. But never forget that the first level of safety is the flyer him/herself. Honesty and awareness about your own skill level and experience can prevent problems that might lead to injury or worse.

Whatever power kiting equipment you've got, check it over frequently for wear and tear. Equipment failure at an inopportune moment, especially out on the water, up in the mountains and/or up in the air, could have serious consequences. Take or send faulty or damaged equipment back to your dealer or the manufacturer. All Flexifoil kites and other equipment are guaranteed against faulty manufacture or unexplained failure. That's not an invitation to trash your kite to bits and expect it to be repaired or replaced free of charge. There are clauses about 'normal wear and tear' in all guarantees and retailers and manufacturers are

eagle-eyed. They can spot mistreatment a mile off. Look after your equipment and it will look after you. Get repairs done without delay. In any event, money spent on a repair could be a life-saver and you can't put a price on that.

Safety is more than just a personal issue though. A little carelessness or over enthusiasm could mean you crash your kite into or onto other kiters, spectators and passers by. While many power kites are, in principle, soft (no rigid frame parts) they can, as we have said, generate enormous power and cause serious injury. But it's not just the kite itself that can be dangerous. Between you and the kite can be anything up to 45 metres or 150 feet of flying lines moving quickly through the air under extreme tension. The flying lines are thin, made from high-quality, light-weight materials to reduce drag and make the kites more efficient. This is a potentially fatal combination as, when flying a reasonable-sized power kite, the effect of the speed, pull and tension gives the lines a cutting capability not far short of cheese wire. There are plenty of stories of careless power kiters losing fingertips to their flying lines. Always disable your kite and flying lines on the ground when you are not using them as an escaped kite dragging its line behind it can be almost as dangerous.

It's your responsibility as the flyer to make sure you have adequate space for whatever power kite sport you're doing. Simply to fly a kite you must allow a clear space downwind of where you're standing – at

least twice the length of your flying lines – to allow for being pulled forward, especially during the launch phase, and a similar amount of space to each side. If people come too close or stand under the kite(s) while you're flying you must fly your kite to a safe place (at the 'zenith' above your head, or landed) and either ask them to move or move yourself until it's safe to fly again. You might want to think about taking out some kind of public indemnity or liability insurance in case of accident. Many clubs and associations offer this as part of their membership and, for anything more than recreational flying, we recommend that you take out appropriate cover.

There are some other 'contra-indications' for kiting. The kites and flying lines are excellent for 'earthing' lightning, so at the first flash of lightning or rumble of thunder get your kite down as fast as possible. Likewise, the kite that dumps itself in the electricity lines will not only fry itself and possibly the flyer, it will quite conceivably short out the national grid and could land you with a hefty fine from the electricity company. Don't fly anywhere near power lines, or next to roads and railways. And be aware that, kite flying of any description is totally prohibited within 5 miles of any airport or field.

All Flexifoil power kites come with operating instructions and a safety warning notice.

▲ Flexifoil Sabre and Blade traction kites have complex bridle / shroud lines to hold their shape
▶ Essential safety information

1 Never fly near overhead power lines, airports, roads or railways.

2 Never fly in thunder storms.

3 Always select a safe launching and landing area away from people and obstacles.

4 Always use appropriate safety equipment.

5 Disable you kite and lines when not in use.

6 Never allow inexperienced kite fliers to use your equipment.

READ AND REMOVE THIS LABEL BEFORE FLIGHT

Ⓢ **FLEXIFOIL**
ORIGINAL FLEXIFOIL POWER KITE

WARNING! ACHTUNG! ATTENTION!

READ THE INSTRUCTIONS THAT COME WITH THE POWER KITE.

NEVER FLY NEAR POWER LINES, IN STORMS, NEAR AIRPORTS OR ROADS. KEEP YOUR FLYING AREA CLEAR OF PEOPLE. DO NOT FLY A POWER KITE WHICH IS TOO BIG FOR YOUR CAPABILITY. DO NOT FLY IN TOO STRONG A WIND. USE PROTECTIVE CLOTHING. POWER KITES CANNOT BE USED FOR PARAGLIDING OR PARASCENDING. YOU ARE RESPONSIBLE FOR THE SAFE OPERATION OF YOUR KITE.

DE NE JAMAIS FAIRE VOLER UN CERF-VOLANT A PLUS DE 100 M. DE HAUTEUR, NI PAR TEMPS D'ORAGE, DE NE JAMAIS VOUS PLACER A PROXIMITE DE LIGNES ELECTRIQUES OU D'UN AEROPORT. QUE POUR LES CERF-VOLANTS DIRIGEABLES 60 M. DE FIL SUFFISENT AMPLEMENT.

DRACHEN NICHT IM GEWITTER, NICHT IN DER NÄHE VON HOCHSPANNUNGSLEITUNGEN, NICHT IN FLUGHAVENNÄHE, NICHT MIT ÜBER 100 M. LANGER SCHNUR FLIEGEN LASSEN!

●フライトに際しては、常に安全を心がけ、細心の注意を払って下さい。高圧線、電線の近くや、雷雨暴風の中 飛行場や交通の混みあった中 通路の近くでは、飛ばさないで下さい。
●フレキンフォイルパワーカイトはかなりの力が出ますので 小型のホ　トンヨット4 以外はお客様には危険です

Read them well before you take your kite out for the first time. There are some specific safety rules that apply to kiteboarding, snowkiting and buggying which we'll cover in those chapters.

One final safety thought. With the exception of when you're using kites for getting airs, when it's recommended you hang on to the controls at all times, your ultimate safety mechanism is to let go completely of the control handles or bar if you feel that it's all getting too much. The kite should be retained by an appropriate safety leash, either that or it will blow away downwind and eventually come to ground without the retaining tension on the flying lines. Letting go without a leash really is a final solution and all other efforts should be made to control the kites first. A released power kite can present a potentially enormous danger to other kiters or bystanders, not to mention leaving you a lot of sorting out before you can fly again. Never attempt to stop an escaped kite by grabbing the flying line, it can cut deep into your hand. In many of the extreme power kite disciplines, where the biggest power is needed, quick release safety systems and leashes are now standard, precisely so that you *can* let the kite go and recover it again without risk to yourself or others.

◀ 10.5 m2 Flexifoil Blade high performance power kite
▶ Flags make great indicators of wind strength and direction

WIND SPEEDS

If you're just starting out with power kites or are just in it for a bit of recreational fun, a simplistic understanding may well be enough. There's either enough wind to fly or not and if there is enough, is there just enough to get the kite up or is it strong enough to make it good fun? In fact it's a popular misconception of our time that you need a tree-snapping wind to fly kites. Normally, most kites will fly well in 10mph or more of wind. If you're getting a bit more specialised and power kiting means getting in your buggy or out on your board as often as possible, then a little more wind strength detail may well be needed to get you sufficiently powered-up. For instance, you'll almost certainly have more than one size of kite depending on what the wind strength is. In a light wind (10mph or knots) you will need to fly a big kite (a 6.0 or 8.0 m² ram air foil, for example) to achieve decent speed in a buggy. The same kite in a big wind (20+mph or knots) will be an uncontrollable monster and potential killer. You need a smaller kite to achieve the same power, a 2, 3 or 4 m² perhaps. Not surprising really, it's the same principle as sailing and windsurfing: big sail = light wind, small sail = strong wind. Bear in mind though that smaller kites tend to fly faster and be more responsive, and they'll be moving faster because of the strong wind too. The more serious you get, the more kites you'll have so that you can always max. your fun whatever the wind.

All good kites come with recommended wind ranges for optimum performance, which you should take good account of.

Flying outside those wind ranges might cause damage to your kite or yourself. A set of kites with overlapping wind ranges will cover you for every eventuality.

Kite wind ranges are normally expressed in wind speeds. There are numerous different ways of measuring wind speed: Beaufort (force 1, 2, 3 etc. as on the shipping forecast), miles per hour, kilometres per hour, knots, metres per second… Understanding these and what is the right range for your kite is one thing, actually measuring it on the day you're out flying is another altogether. There are a few ways of doing this. First, watch the weather forecast on television, they usually give forecasted wind speeds (in mph in the UK) in a circle on the chart, with a little arrow attached to show direction, but these are very general. You could try the Met Office website for a more detailed view of a particular spot. A better and more accurate way would be to buy yourself a pocket wind meter to measure the wind on site, but you'll need to spend a decent amount of money to get anything remotely accurate. If you're sailing from a centre or club they normally have a high- quality anemometer on site giving a constant and accurate reading.

A less scientific but nonetheless useful method is to look for wind indicators in the environment; they can give you an enormous amount of information. Watch for smoke or clouds in the sky, flags and

▶ For handling big power, riders often use a control bar and harness

trees moving, sand lifting on the beach, the surface of water for rippling, white horses, waves etc. There's a table on page 23 which shows all the official measures and a list of indicators you can use. One thing to be aware of is the arrival of big, dark, stormy clouds. These fronts almost always bring with them a big wind surge as they arrive that can be extremely dangerous. If in doubt try to land your kite before the front hits.

With time you'll learn to 'feel' the wind and make your decision on which kite to use from your experience. You'll know instinctively when to switch to a smaller or bigger kite from your muscle and brain memory of similar situations. One thing you do need to understand is that there's a point at which power kiting becomes dangerous however you're doing it. Watch what the serious flyers and riders do. When conditions are too extreme they stay indoors. As a rough guide, anything over Force 6 (30 mph) is going to start making things very exciting to the point of dangerous. Power kiting in more than force 8 (40 mph) is really not recommended, even with the most sophisticated kite and safety systems in the world.

There are a couple of other factors to consider as well. Your flying lines can make a big difference to how the kite performs in different wind speeds. It's all a question of weight, diameter, stretch, the kind of activity you're doing and the drag that results from that combination of factors. Modern power kite flying lines are made of materials that significantly reduce all three factors but you

WIND SPEED

WIND SPEED INDICATORS (PROBABLE)

Force	MPH	Knots	KPH	Metres/sec	Description	At sea	On land
0	<1	<1	<1	0–0.2	Calm	Smooth as glass	Calm; smoke rises vertically
1	1–3	1–3	1–5	0.3–1.5	Light Air	Ripples with no appearance of scales; no foam crests	Smoke drift indicates wind direction; vanes do not move
2	4–7	4–6	6–11	1.6–3.3	Light Breeze	Small wavelets; crests of glassy appearance	Wind felt on face; leaves rustle; vanes begin to move
3	8–12	7–10	12–19	3.4–5.4	Gentle Wind	Large wavelets; crests begin to break, scattered white caps	Leaves and small twigs in motion; light flags extended
4	13–18	11–16	20–29	5.5–7.9	Moderate Wind	1–4ft waves; numerous whitecaps	Leaves and loose paper raised up; flags flap; small branches move
5	19–24	17–21	30–38	8.0–10.7	Fresh Wind	4–8ft waves; many whitecaps; some spray	Small trees begin to sway; flags flap and ripple
6	25–31	22–27	39–50	10.8–13.8	Strong Wind	8-–13ft waves forming white caps everywhere; more spray	Large branches in motion; whistling heard in wires
7	32–38	28–33	51–61	13.9–17.1	Near Gale	13–20ft waves; white foam blown in streaks	Whole trees in motion; resistance felt in walking against wind
8	39–46	34–40	62–74	17.2–20.7	Gale	13–20ft waves; edges of crests beginning to break; foam in streaks	Whole trees in motion; resistance felt in walking against wind (again)
9	47–54	41–47	75–86	20.8–24.4	Strong Gale	20ft waves; sea begins to roll; dense streaks of foam	Slight structural damage occurs; shingles blow from roofs
10	55–63	48–55	87–101	24.5–28.4	Storm	20–30ft waves; white churning sea; rolling is heavy; reduced visibility	Trees broken/uprooted; considerable structural damage occurs

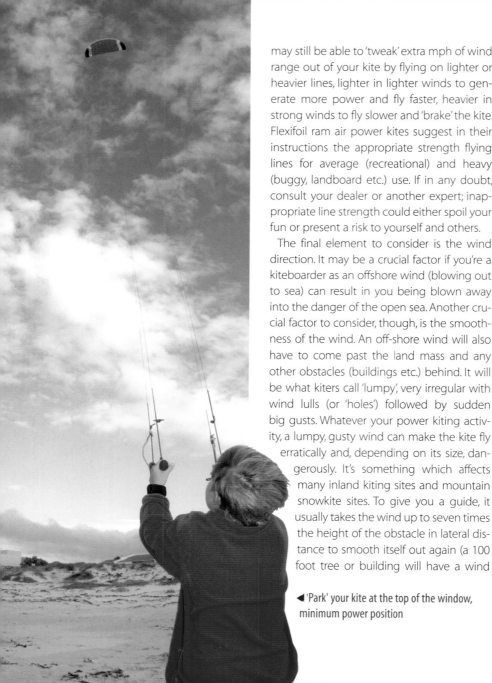

may still be able to 'tweak' extra mph of wind range out of your kite by flying on lighter or heavier lines, lighter in lighter winds to generate more power and fly faster, heavier in strong winds to fly slower and 'brake' the kite. Flexifoil ram air power kites suggest in their instructions the appropriate strength flying lines for average (recreational) and heavy (buggy, landboard etc.) use. If in any doubt, consult your dealer or another expert; inappropriate line strength could either spoil your fun or present a risk to yourself and others.

The final element to consider is the wind direction. It may be a crucial factor if you're a kiteboarder as an offshore wind (blowing out to sea) can result in you being blown away into the danger of the open sea. Another crucial factor to consider, though, is the smoothness of the wind. An off-shore wind will also have to come past the land mass and any other obstacles (buildings etc.) behind. It will be what kiters call 'lumpy', very irregular with wind lulls (or 'holes') followed by sudden big gusts. Whatever your power kiting activity, a lumpy, gusty wind can make the kite fly erratically and, depending on its size, dangerously. It's something which affects many inland kiting sites and mountain snowkite sites. To give you a guide, it usually takes the wind up to seven times the height of the obstacle in lateral distance to smooth itself out again (a 100 foot tree or building will have a wind

◄ 'Park' your kite at the top of the window, minimum power position

turbulence 'shadow' up to 700 feet long). It doesn't make kiting impossible but it can make it much more difficult. Whatever your location, find the most open, exposed site you can and position yourself as far downwind of any obstacles as possible. Beach sites are great for most kinds of power kiting because, apart from the space you have available to use, often, with an onshore blowing from the sea, or side wind blowing along the beach, the wind is smooth and controlling the kite is much easier because it behaves consistently. Gusty, irregular wind will make your learning process much longer.

THE WIND WINDOW

Anyone who's come to power kiting from another wind sport might be more familiar with the term 'wind envelope'. It's the actual field of manoeuvre described by the kite on the end of its flying lines as it moves around the sky with the flyer standing still, and it dictates how much and what type of power your kite will generate. That's an important consideration because, put simply, most kite traction sports rely on moving the kite with power to one side of the window to pull you in that direction.

Try a quick wind window test for yourself; here's a limit to each side of you and how far above your head you can fly the kite to before it either stops moving and/or loses power, stalls and falls out of the sky. With you as a fixed point at its centre, the wind window described resembles the surface of a quarter sphere. There really isn't any kite that can make the full quarter sphere, which requires a full 180 degree lateral pass, but a well powered up Flexifoil Proteam 8 or Super 10 kite will come very close. Most kites are nearer 130 to 140 degrees as an average. The illustration below will help you understand. Bear in mind too that the wind can shift and change direction. When that happens your orientation must shift with the wind until you relocate the new window centre and edges. Wind shifts can happen for various reasons, responding to tides, affected by landmass, land heating up during the day…

Power kites are normally most efficient when they're at the centre of the wind window, flying horizontally across the sky at roughly head height or slightly above, 'centre window'. Here they move fastest and pull hardest. Keep flying horizontally and the kite will gradually slow down and lose power as it reaches the 'edge' of its window. Turn the kite round and fly back across the wind window. As you reach the window centre turn upwards and fly the kite straight up. If the wind is strong enough you'll notice yourself being pulled by a rush of power, followed by the same slowing down and de-powering effect until the kite reaches a 'parked' position up above your head. This is known as the zenith or 'safety' position. There's almost no power in the kite up here and it's the place to try and steer the kite if you ever feel you're getting into difficulties.

Flying a big power kite near the centre of the window will generate enormous lateral pull and this is where you'll find yourself lean-ing right back, even lying down, to stop yourself being pulled over and dragged along on your front. In fact you rarely see landboarders, buggy drivers or kiteboarders fly their big kites near centre window because the lateral pull would be too much to hold, leading to a big horizontal wipe out. What they do is use a different part of the wind window to generate the kind of power that is most useful to them. In addition, once you start using the wind to move along, whichever way you do it, there's a factor called 'apparent wind' you'll need to deal with. It has an effect on the wind direction and strength and is fully explained in Chapter 5 – 'Let's get moving'.

As with wind speeds, how its position in the wind window affects your kite is something that's worth understanding in principle but will become much more intuitive with experience. Your skill as a flyer will be in learning how to manipulate the kite in the wind window to deliver the kind and quantity of pull you want. Generally speaking, flying at either the top or bottom end of a kite's wind range will give you a smaller (narrower and lower) wind window. In light winds you'll need to really 'work' the kite near the edges, even in centre window, to achieve real power. In the middle of the kite's wind range you'll generally find that the kite has a bigger wind window and has strong pull over a much bigger area of the window.

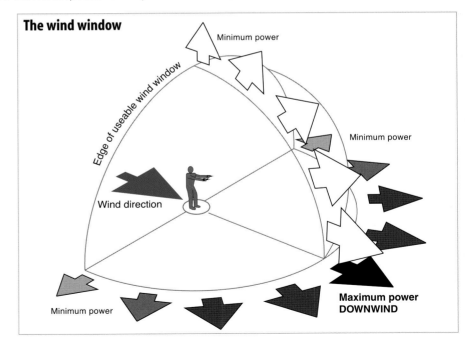

The wind window

Minimum power

Edge of useable wind window

Minimum power

Wind direction

Minimum power

Maximum power DOWNWIND

TWO LINE

3

"My first power kite was a 6' Stacker, I was amazed at the power and speed that generated, but it wasn't long before I'd bought 4 Super 10s to stack and really discovered the awesome power of the wind.

MIKE SHAW, FLEXIFOIL INTERNATIONAL SALES MANAGER AND POWER KITE FANATIC

27

RECREATIONAL FLYING

Recreational flying covers just about everything that isn't one of the extreme power kite disciplines, let's say, the kind of flying where you don't really need extra safety equipment, flying your kite for nothing more than the simple but satisfying pleasure of controlling it as you fly it around the sky and feeling something of what kite power can be from it pulling on your arms. If you're a complete beginner or the kind of person who likes to keep your kites in the car to use occasionally, when there's a good wind blowing, you're a recreational flyer. If, on the other hand, you like to get out as often as possible with the biggest rig possible that's appropriate for the conditions, with the added spice of big jumps, fast buggying or carving some serious sand, surf or snow, then you're an altogether different proposition.

Most people trying power kiting for the first time or starting to fly regularly do indeed start on a Flexifoil power kite. It usually starts by going out with a friend who's already converted to kite power and having a go on theirs. The second step normally comes the day afterwards when you hunt down your nearest power kite dealer (there's a list of recommended Flexifoil dealers available at www.flexifoil.com) and buy yourself a kite

◀ Flexifoil kites are simple to stack
▶ Flexifoil's latest two-line development, the Buzz

pronto because, like 99.9% of first timers, you're an instant convert. If your ultimate aim is to take power kiting to its limits, then it's perfectly possible to learn kite skills on one of the big traction kites but you can learn more, much quicker, not to mention have a pile of fun, if you start with one of these fantastic sky-sweeping two line Flexifoil kites. On its 30 metre lines it really fills up the sky, moving fast and pulling hard and few other kites are able to describe the shape and extent of the wind window as well as a 'Flexi'. Its distinctive shape has made it a 'household-name' among power kiters the world over, instantly recognisable flown individually or in the big stacks serious Flexi freaks love so much.

The Stacker 6 was of course Flexifoil's first ever design and its enduring popularity speaks volumes for what a great invention it was, or rather, still is. Overall, Stackers have remained relatively unchanged from the original concept but they've been best sellers for more than 25 years. What makes the Stacker so great is that it's easy to fly, it's fast, it's unbelievably durable, and it gives you a taste of what real kite power can feel like without it ever pulling too hard. And the Stacker is the first of three classic kite-sized steps to big power...

When you're ready (or if you just can't wait) you can jump straight onto the slightly slower moving but seriously heavier pulling bigger kites, step 2 – the Proteam 8, or step 3 – the Super 10', which will give you your first experience of serious kite power. The increase in pull through the wingspans is impressive and with a Super 10' flying in 15mph of good steady wind you'll be getting one of the best workouts you've had in ages. Smaller kites move faster, remember,

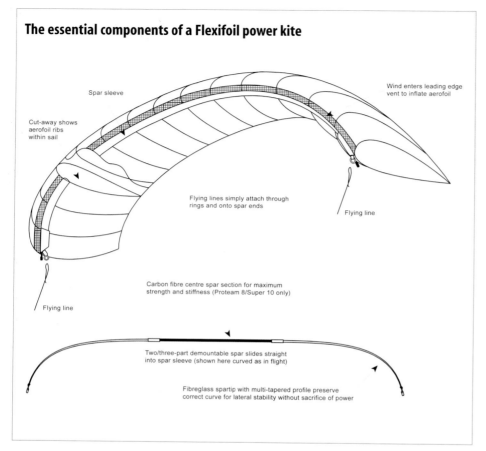

The essential components of a Flexifoil power kite

Spar sleeve

Cut-away shows
aerofoil ribs
within sail

Wind enters leading edge
vent to inflate aerofoil

Flying lines simply attach through
rings and onto spar ends

Flying line

Flying line

Carbon fibre centre spar section for maximum
strength and stiffness (Proteam 8/Super 10 only)

Two/three-part demountable spar slides straight
into spar sleeve (shown here curved as in flight)

Fibreglass spartip with multi-tapered profile preserve
correct curve for lateral stability without sacrifice of power

held flatter in flight by its multiple bridle support lines, still with a noticeable arch shape. It certainly hasn't broken the tradition of successful Flexifoil kites though and, like its predecessors, it's a stable, fun kite, easy to learn on, one which packs down into a small stuff-bag for more convenient carrying in a pocket or backpack. With a Buzz you really can take your kite anywhere. It's got light pull and a huge wind range and wind window, making it very forgiving, a perfect kite for learning, for recreational flying or as a trainer for bigger, more serious kites.

DESCRIPTIONS AND USES

"Simplicity has helped the basic Flexifoil kite remain a popular recreational power kite, but its efficiency and reliability, like all functioning designs, depends on a combination of good conception, suitable materials and quality workmanship."

Andrew Jones, original Flexifoil co-designer

The Flexifoil Stacker was the first and original modern power kite, created 30 years ago. What's more, it has inspired power kite design and manufacture all over the world. People have tried other power kite designs (framed deltas, flat framed sails etc.) but the raw power and unbeatable durability of ram air kites, specially under heavy crashing, meant that the ram air quickly became the overwhelmingly popular power kite form.

Almost all ram air kites follow the same

and the Proteam 8' is the ideal compromise kite, fast through the air like a Stacker 6, plenty of pull like a Super 10 to exercise your muscles. And if you do ultimately progress to extreme power kiting, you'll still keep your old Flexis in your kite bag, because for pure fun flying and for introducing newcomers to the sport, little can beat these first three members of the Flexifoil family.

The most recent addition to Flexifoil's two line recreational kite range has seen them break with tradition by releasing a completely soft air foil starter kite. Unlike the Stacker 6, Proteam 8 and Super 10 with which Flexifoil made their name, it's got no rods or spars to give it its shape. Actually it's got a very different shape from the classic, arched Flexi. The wing has a deeper section and the sail is

construction techniques and principles as a Flexifoil kite, which is best described as a tethered (to you, the flyer) aerofoil kite or wing. It's similar in basic structure to a modern parachute or paraglider. The kite is essentially two rectangular pieces of fabric held together lengthways and separated to give it a three dimensional shape by a series of carefully shaped fabric ribs between the two sheets. The kite shape is critical as it dictates the amount of lift and pull delivered. The internal ribs divide the kite wing into sections, called cells. The kite is sealed at the rear (trailing) edge but the front (leading) edge has openings to allow the wind to inflate it. On many kites the vents are covered with gauze which lets the wind in but keeps unwanted rubbish out. Once inflated the kite takes on an aerofoil profile, that is to say, in cross section it is similar to a conventional aeroplane wing, fat at the front edge tapering to a point at the back. Take a look at the diagram on page 30. Just like an aeroplane wing, it's the difference in speed of airflow over the two surfaces of the wing leading to a corresponding difference in air pressure that generates the power and forward movement (in the case of the moving plane or paraglider this gives it the lift to get up and stay up).

Those of you who've had a look at a paraglider or a parachute will be familiar with the complex structure of 'shroud' lines

▲ The distinctive arched shape of a Flexifoil two line power kite
▶ The reinforced weave of ripstop nylon sailcloth

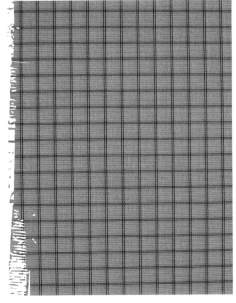

coming from points all over the underside surface of the wing. These usually join together at two points, one on each side of the wing, and these two points are what the pilot's harness attaches to, usually hanging a little way below on two extension lines. It's the same on a soft ram air kite like the Buzz, except that the 'pilot' is 20 or more metres away on the end of the flying lines standing still on the ground, rather than hanging underneath hundreds of feet up in the air.

Ordinarily, soft aerofoil kites need a similar complex bridle or shroud line structure to hold their shape once in flight, otherwise they could collapse in on themselves. Kites such as the Buzz, Sting and many of the big traction kites that we'll be looking at later are exactly that kind. But the beauty of the Flexifoil idea is its simplicity. This was almost accidentally achieved – Jones and Merry were unaware of other existing soft aerofoil wings with complex shroud lines, so invented their own system, one where there's very little that can ever go wrong. A classic Flexifoil kite has its single, flexible, tapered rod that fits into a pocket running across the leading (front) edge of the kite. This is what keeps the sail spread out in the correct shape to fly. The rod, which formed a crucial part of the Flexifoil patent and helped ensure their product's uniqueness, also helps the kite self-adjust its angle of attack against the wind, pivoting around the spar in different areas of the wind window and under different degrees of power. The sail tips and the control lines are attached to the tips of this rod. Once inflated and with the tension of the

control lines fixed to you, the flyer, the kite has an irresistible need to move forwards and it's up to you to pilot it around the sky. As mentioned earlier, as much as any other factor, the rod's strong, stiff centre and flexible tips give Flexifoil kites their classic arched shape in the sky. That curve or arch of the kite is another critical factor in their functioning.

The sail fabric itself is sail cloth nylon, as used on yachting sails and commonly known as 'ripstop'. It was the obvious choice really, having all the qualities required to complete the Flexifoil formula: lightweight, tough, durable, non-porous, low stretch, proven performance in wind sports. Ripstop comes in many grades or weights and for early power kites the lightest one was selected, spinnaker nylon. In time, kite industry demands were great enough that fabric manufacturers began to make ripstop specifically for kites. All Flexifoil kites (6, 8, 10 and Buzz included) are now made from Chikara ripstop nylon, specifically woven for kite manufacture. The excellent colour ranges available mean that there's always a good choice of kite colour options, so Flexifoil kites always look great, an important consideration as, hopefully, you're going to spend a lot of time watching them up there in the sky.

The bigger, Proteam 8 and Super 10, kites use the same basic design and materials – nylon sail with a rod across the front – with

▲ Relaxed flying position (elbows in, hands close and low) and the perfect flying spot
◀ Flying lines attach directly to wing tips (left)
▶ Spar in its pocket or sleeve

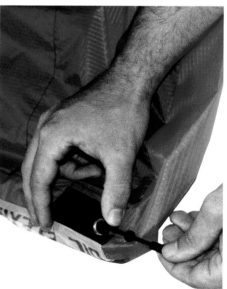

some modifications. The bigger kites have longer, stronger rods and, where the Stacker has 10 cells across its span, the Proteam 8 has 14 and the Super 10 has18. 'Bolting on' extra cells or sail area affects something called the 'aspect ratio', the ratio of the depth to the span. Lower aspect ratios (the Stacker) tend to be more stable, higher aspect ratios (more elongated like the Super 10) more efficient with higher performance. Finding the perfect balance is the kite designer's skill, – making sure that although different, all kite sizes handle similarly.

Flown singly or in stacks, Flexifoils are ideal for learning how to handle power kites and can be used for taking your first steps in kite traction: body dragging, getting airs etc. It's possible to use stacked Flexifoils for more extreme power kite sports but by no means as easy as if you use one of the kites designed specifically for that. Although an adult toy recommended for ages 12 and upwards, children under 12 are perfectly capable of flying them (kids usually learn much faster than adults) but will need adult supervision in case the kite starts to pull too much. For sheer speed through the sky nothing can beat a Flexifoil Stacker 6, and that's official. 110mph has been clocked, a figure you're very welcome to try and surpass. The Proteam 8 takes you to the realm of kite traction, enough to start pulling an average-build person around. The Super 10 is the undisputed best selling power kite

in the world. Awesome power, steady in flight, easy control, the kite to test your skill and muscles to the max.

The Buzz is different in that one crucial area, the fact that it has no stiffening rods to hold the kite in shape. The Buzz has a more complex paraglider-style bridle structure, as described earlier. Bridle points are spread across the whole underside of the kite, leading to two flying line attachment points, ensure the kite keeps its shape and profile, helping to make it super stable right across the wind window and to give it a wide operating wind range. A 'limiter' line running between the two toggle attachment points helps prevent the kite folding in on itself in light winds. The cell structure is similar to the classic Flexifoil kites but with a deeper rib section profile, giving the kite much more internal volume, and the shape is different too, more semi-eliptical than the classic oblong Flexifoil. The bridle is made from sleeved Dyneema line making it very strong and reducing weight and drag from the multiple bridle lines. It packs down into a convenient, small, wide-vented stuff bag. One thing you won't be able to do with a Buzz, however, is to stack it as you can with the classic Flexifoils, to get extra power.

Serious power kites now come with sophisticated harnesses, de-power systems and quick release safety systems, to reduce the risks of dealing with the immense power required, for instance on the water. This has enabled competitors as young as 11 years old not simply to enter but win international kiteboarding contests for adults. The equipment adapts itself to

▲ How to wear wrist straps
▶ A Flexifoil Super 10 'Stealth'

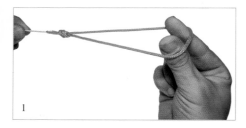

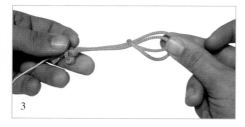

▲ The lark's head knot explained

rider size: smaller kites and boards for smaller riders, the same models but bigger for bigger riders. In the correct circumstances there's absolutely no reason why children shouldn't enjoy the thrills of power kiting too. Don't be scared, but be very, very careful.

That message applies to everyone, not just children. If you want to enjoy extreme kite power, completely mastering basic power kites can be an important stage. You may quickly get bored with the simplicity but there may be times in the future when your understanding of how kites fly and the wind window in which they do so will give you the kind of intuition that could later save crucial 1/100ths of a second to make a decision that could either endanger or save your life.

SET UP AND PACK UP PROCEDURE

When you buy your first Flexifoil kite or Buzz, you are thoroughly recommended to take your new toy home, read the instruction manual, un-pack it, familiarise yourself with its anatomy (!) and re-pack it again at least once in the calm of your living room **before** you head off to your nearest flying site for a blast. Standing in a windy field trying to read the manual and control the flapping nylon sail at the same time is not conducive to happy power kiting. Reading the instructions you'll become aware of how simple these kites are to prepare for action. Once you're familiar with the proce-

dure it'll quickly become automatic. Follow the instructions and you can't really go wrong. And if you do, take the kite back to your local dealer for some advice. There's no assembly required for the Buzz, of course, but you still need to know which way to set it up to be able to take off and where to attach your lines.

With the kite out of its bag and/or fully assembled it's time to head back to your equipment bag for your flying or control lines and pre-attached wrist straps. First, take the flying lines. There are two lines packed together on one line winder and they're ready to use with a 'sleeved' loop on each end of each line. The quality of the lines you use can make a huge difference to the efficiency, response and general flying of the kite. Nowadays all Flexifoil power kites come with Dyneema flying lines to give you the best possible performance from your kite. Dyneema is a synthetic fibre, specially braided to make flying lines which are strong, lightweight, low diameter, with less than 5% stretch and very slippery. They enable kites to fly more efficiently with minimal drag and once 'flown in' (a few hours of flying pulls any remaining stretch out) give a 'fly by wire' feel of immediate response. Conventional nylon or polyester lines are heavier, fatter and have up to 20% stretch. Flexifoil-recommended line packs are always Dyneema. One word of warning, however. Don't try to tie knots directly into a Dyneema line. Their chemical make up gives them a low melting point and explains the need for a Dacron sleeve at each end, where the attachment knots are tied. Unsleeved Dyneema will soon rub up enough friction heat to cut clean through itself. If you break a line that means replacing it, or even the whole set!

To attach a Flexifoil kite to its lines, unwind a few metres of both lines, separate them and take one end to each kite tip. Put the looped end of line through the metal ring at the sail tip and pull a little excess line through with it. Now make a lark's head knot in the looped end, as shown on page 34 in our step by step instructions (this is the single most useful knot in power kiting so learn it now). Place the lark's head knot between the grommet and end cap on the spar and pull it tight, as shown in your instructions. Pull the excess line you needed to make the knot back through the metal ring towards the line winder. The great thing about the lark's head is that it's a slip knot: the harder you pull it the tighter it locks, so once correctly attached and under tension from the kite there's no chance it can come off in flight. Once tension is released though (after landing) it's easy to loosen and detach.

The Buzz is simpler to set up. There's no metal ring to pass your lines through, just two attachment points, one each side where all the bridle lines come together, in the form of small line toggles with knot-heads at the end. Make sure the bridle is not twisted or

tangled and lay the kite on its back, across the wind, open vents pointing downwind and the trailing edge weighted down with sand or a backpack, making sure you don't snag any of the bridle lines. The Buzz flying lines are in fact pre-attached, using the same lark's head knot as explained earlier. In your instructions you'll find an explanation of how to remove and re-attach your lines should you wish. Undo the lines from their retaining croc grips on the trailing edge and unwind your lines upwind.

When you've unwound the lines (put the empty winder somewhere you know you'll find it again) you'll find that at the other end your flying straps are pre-attached. Look closely and you'll also see that they are attached with a lark's head knot, albeit tied a slightly different way, the loop on the end of the line passing through the plastic attachment ring on the wrist straps, then the strap passed back through the loop and pulled securely tight.

Anyway, that's quite enough waffle, you'll be pleased to hear that the real fun is just about to begin…

HOW TO LAUNCH, FLY AND LAND

"The most common beginner mistakes you see are people not keeping their backs to the wind, swinging round 90 degrees with the pull of the kite and flying themselves right out of the window. That and not fully

▲ Assisted launch
▶ Two solo launch techniques

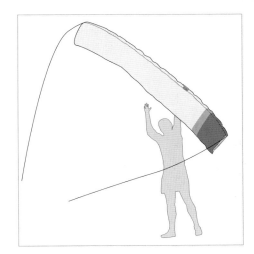

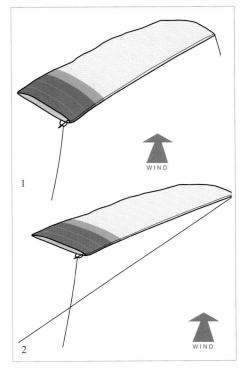

unwinding the lines before launch : not only will the kite be un-powered, the lines will be different lengths and it'll be much harder to fly."

'Andreya Wharry – Flexifoil International team kiteboarder, Extreme Academy power kite instructor

Launching the kite

Launching any of these recreational kites can be done solo or with a helper. Let's look at the assisted launch first.

■ Position yourself so that the kite is as directly downwind of you as possible with your flying lines attached and untwisted and the appropriate line going to each hand. Adopt a good body position, hands in the 'handlebar' position, just in front of your torso, arms slightly bent and elbows tucked in, knees slightly flexed ready for the kite to launch and start pulling.

■ If you're launching a Flexifoil kite your helper should hold the kite in the centre of its leading edge by the spar which they will feel through the pocket, making sure that the kite is the right way up (gauze opening above the spar) and taking care not to block the vents with their hand. Have them hold the kite above their head and wait for it to fully inflate. Launching a Buzz, your helper should stand behind the kite and hold the top of the leading edge so that the vents are open and the kite is able to inflate.

◀ Flexifoil Buzz, great for learning the basics

When you're sure the kite's ready and there's enough wind, call to your helper to release the kite. They shouldn't try to 'throw' the kite into the air, you should fly out of their hand, straight up the wind window. In lighter wind you may need to take a few steps backward at the moment of launch to help the kite up into stronger wind. Avoid lifting your hands and arms to encourage the kite to climb, this actually makes controlling the kite more difficult. Keep your elbows in, ready to start steering.

We'll look at steering in a moment but first let's quickly run through solo launching. With a Flexifoil kite there are two ways, both requiring a bit of preparation of the kite.

- First way: position the kite the right way up on the ground but at an angle, not straight on to the wind but less than perpendicular, as shown in the photo. When you pull the kite straight by pulling gently on the line attached to the furthest tip, it will inflate and get ready to lift off.

- Second way (may be better in very strong wind): lay the kite down at an angle to the wind as before, but upside down (gauze below the spar). This time you will need a sharp pull on the furthest tip to flip the kite over so it can inflate. It will need a good tug to spin it round, then give it time for the wind to open up and inflate the sail.

▶ Top: Left loop
Middle: Right loop
Bottom: Looping crosses wraps your lines, loop back the other way to unwrap

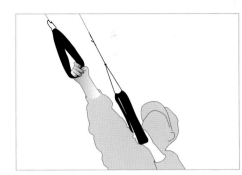

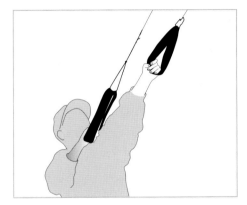

- Whichever way you get the kite into the correct position, once it's inflated you will probably need to walk smoothly backwards a few paces to get it to lift off. Avoid hard tugging, this actually impedes launch.

Like anything, practice makes perfect so persevere if you don't get either launch straight off. Solo launching is easier on a hard, sandy beach than a park or playing field, where the kite or lines can snag on the grass. In good wind the kite should lift off on its own, but you may need to help it up the first few metres. Don't jerk with your arms: pull back by walking – even running – slowly, steadily and smoothly backwards. Losing a few metres backwards is no problem as, all being well, you're going to be pulled forwards again once the kite's flying. If it doesn't launch fairly quickly go and set it up and try again. Dragging or yanking the kite across the ground too much is a sure way of damaging it. Use the assisted launch if needed.

Solo launching a Buzz is altogether simpler. Lying on its back with the trailing edge weighted down the kite will stay in place while you put the wrist straps on and prepare to launch.

- Take up the tension slowly on both lines, lifting the leading edge off the ground and opening the vents to the wind. Hold the kite in this position and allow it to inflate properly.

- Once the kite is inflated pull it gently and evenly with both lines until the weight falls off the trailing edge and the kite lifts off.

Steering the kite

If you can steer a bike or a car you can fly a power kite. The main thing, as with your car or bike, is to keep your movements as smooth as possible and avoid steering jerkily. When you launch the kite it will fly straight up into the sky (if this doesn't happen check the troubleshooting section which follows). You can either wait until it reaches a hover or parked position above your head to start steering it (you'll have to watch out that you don't over-fly and drop the kite out of the sky) or preferably take control of it before it reaches the top of the wind window, thereby keeping it powered-up and moving, the thing Two line power kites like best. Remember that the stronger the wind the quicker the kite flies and the

▲ Leaning against the pull puts you in ideal shape for controlled skids

faster your reactions will need to be. Try in a moderate wind first until you're feeling really confident…

- As the kite reaches three-quarters of the way up the wind window, pull back a short distance (6" or so), smoothly and firmly on the right line. The kite flies to the right.

- Correct your steering by bringing your hands parallel again then pull similarly on the left line. The kite flies to the left.

- Correct your steering again and the kite flies straight up the wind window to a hover ('zenith' position) above your head.

You can spend a bit of time moving backwards and forwards across the sky like that if you like but it's more interesting to start doing some loops. With the kite in centre window near the top…

- Pull steadily on the right line, this time keeping the pull going so that the kite

flies to the right and then describes a circle downwards to the right. Don't pull too hard and put the kite into a really tight spin which tends to 'stall' it. A wider, smooth turn is best, enough to bring the kite round in a complete loop, the bottom of which should be a good few metres above the ground. A combined pull with the right and push with the left (about 6" each hand for a Stacker or Buzz, more with a bigger, stronger-pulling kite), just like on a bike, makes the smoothest turn. Keep pulling on the right line until the kite comes round and it's pointing straight up the window again.

- As the kite comes round full circle and is pointing straight up the wind window, correct your steering and it will fly straight up.

At this point your lines are crossed over each other, but don't worry, a half twist like that makes almost no difference to the controls of the kite. Don't cross your hands to compensate; to untwist the lines all you need to do is let the kite climb up towards the top of the window again, then…

- Pull on the left line hard and long enough to bring the kite round in a complete loop to the left, as you did to the right before, at the end of which, if you bring your hands parallel, it should be once again pointing straight up the wind window, roughly in the centre, flying lines untwisted.

- As the kite comes up the wind window again it's up to you, right or left loop, and so on…

Congratulations! You've just made the first

steps towards being a capable power kite flyer, embarking on a potentially long and fun-filled journey, exploring the amazing world of wind and kite power. Relax and enjoy your flying, start to play with wider and tighter loops and spins, explore the wind window and get to grips with the big lateral pull low-down. To begin with, keep flying right and left loops, a figure of eight on its side, which gives you a nice continuous pattern you can fly while you really familiarise yourself with how the kite handles. You can fly quite a few loops in one direction before you need to untwist but you will need to at some point. Try to keep a rough count in your head and untwist from time to time.

All Flexifoil power kites are very, very durable, which is just as well because almost certainly you'll have some big wipe-outs to begin with, crashing the kites hard into the ground. It's a big laugh, especially when someone else does it, but try and keep your crashes to a minimum as repeated 'unintentional ground contacts' will spoil and eventually damage the kite.

One other manoeuvre you will certainly want to try is a horizontal pass or sweep which, with practice, you'll be able to make closer and closer to the ground. Let's start with a right to left sweep.

- Pull on the right line as if to make a big right loop taking the kite down to the bottom quarter of the wind window.

- Now it's all a question of timing and it may take a few goes to get it right. Instead of completing the loop, when the kite's leading edge is pointing *across* the wind win-

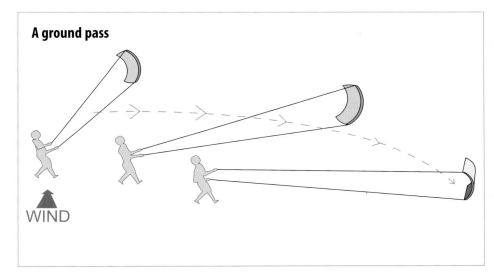

A ground pass

WIND

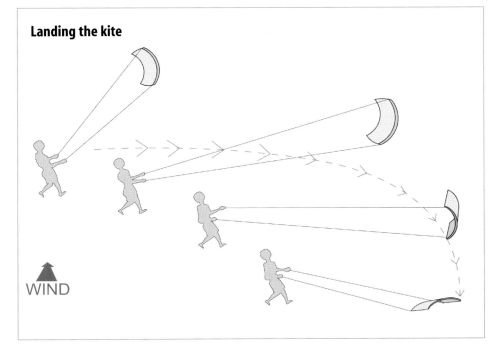

Landing the kite

WIND

dow bring your hands almost parallel, right hand slightly above the left, and fly the kite across the wind window from right to left.

■ The kite will power up through the centre of the window. As it starts to slow down on the left side of the window, pull again on your right line so the kite U-turns until it's pointing across the window, going back the way it came. Bring your hands almost parallel again but with the left above the right and fly a pass back the other way.

Simply reverse the above swapping left for right to fly a pass in the opposite direction. Soon you'll be confident enough to try those impressive ground-skimming sweeps, always watching out for other fliers and stray passers by, of course.

LANDING THE KITE

Sooner or later you're going to get tired, especially if you're flying a Proteam 8 or Super 10, and want to land the kite or pass it on to someone else. In the latter case it's very simple. Fly your kite up to top centre of the window, the 'park' position, slip your wrists out of the straps and pass them quickly to the next flyer. But even so, eventually you'll need to land (you may need to eat or sleep!). Do not fly a fully-inflated, powered-up kite straight into the ground as it may well burst the sail; there's a safe and simple way to do it:

▲ Colour-coded Dyneema flying lines on their winder
◄ Serious damage caused by heavy vents-down landing

■ Put the kite into a horizontal pass as described, low down if you can but that will come with practice.

■ As the kite passes centre window and starts flying towards the minimum power area on the edge, keep it going in that direction.

■ The kite slows down and the pull reduces until eventually the kite flies out of the wind window and falls gently to the ground. You can take a step or two forwards to make sure it settles on the ground if you like.

The kite will normally land upside down. Although it can't take off from that position you should still immobilise it. Peg down one of your flying lines by the wrist straps. That will prevent it re-launching or blowing away in a gust and it will help keep your flying lines in good order. Most good kite shops sell ground stakes but at a push a big tent peg will do the trick. Then go and properly immobilise your kite with sand or a bag, unless you've got a helper who has already done the job for you (in which case off you go to your cool bag to get the nice person a cold beer). A non-abrasive weighted item such as a carry bag or water bottle makes a good kite weight unless you're on the beach, in which case use sand. There are clear instructions with each kite telling you the best way to pack it away. Try to follow these each time to store the kites in good order.

If you can launch, fly the kite without crashing, then land, you're well on the way to being an accomplished power kite flyer. Practise your controls to left and right until you're confident on both sides and understand the mechanics of the wind, then you'll soon be ready to graduate to the serious stuff. That could be flying big stacks, or moving on to the big traction kites for kiteboarding, landboarding or kite buggying. Either way, you'll be joining very good company as one of the many satisfied Flexifoil power kite owners.

TROUBLESHOOTING

It's worth repeating that the beauty of the Flexifoil concept is its simplicity – there's so little that can go wrong. The same applies to the Buzz despite its more complex bridle structure. Nevertheless, you may occasionally find that your kite doesn't seem to be flying properly. If so try checking the following.

The kite flies continually to one side

- Check that both lines are the same length. The best way to do this is to peg the loops at one end to the ground and pull them tight from the other. A quick visual check will show you. If they're unequal you will need to make an adjustment. Undo the loop of the longest line and undo the knots holding the line sleeving in place. Slide the sleeving along until it is equal with the shorter line and retie the knots.

- Check that you and the kite are correctly positioned in the centre of the wind window. If the kite is near the edge it will want to fly towards the centre as soon as it launches.

▶ All-time classic : a stack of Flexis

The power kite 'bounces' violently in flight after launching

- There may be sand or water inside the cells. Land the kite and try and remove the sand through the gauze vent.

- The sail may be very wet (affects smaller models mostly). Dry the sail thoroughly before re-launching.

The wingtips 'flap' during flight

- On a classic Flexifoil kite the sail may be over-stretched on the spar. Move the line attachments 1 to 4 centimetres further in. This may require moving and re-sticking the grommet / stopper (super glue is recommended). Flapping for long periods will eventually damage the fabric.

- The fabric at the wing tips may be worn or damaged.

If you've tried these solutions and the kite still won't perform go straight back to your dealer or contact Flexifoil International direct. The problem could be a manufacturing fault but it could equally be a simple mistake you're making.

The kites are guaranteed against faulty manufacture but not against faulty flying. Kites may well end up getting damaged and Flexifoil run an excellent and reasonably priced repair service, which you can use via your dealer or direct. You can make small sail repairs yourself with a repair kit from your Flexifoil dealer. Larger tears (anything more than an inch or so) should be sent away for repair straight away. Check

your kite over regularly and get repairs carried out quickly.

Keep an eye on the spar sections, too; the carbon centres for the Proteam 8 and Super 10 should not be roughly handled as they can chip and weaken if knocked. Running without a repair to sail or spar is inviting bigger trouble later and may put your personal safety at risk. And you'll have to face the fact that if you really hammer your kite – flying day in – day out, for long periods, especially in bright sunlight with its harmful ultra violet rays – it (the sail fabric primarily) is going to deteriorate and wear out completely one day. Hey, nothing lasts forever!

STACKING

Stacking is the common term given to the

linking together and simultaneous flying of two or more power kites on one set of control lines (also known as flying in 'train'). Flexifoil's classic Stacker 6, Proteam 8 and Super 10 kites are virtually unique in that they can be easily 'stacked' in this way. Different sized Flexifoils can even be stacked together, although it works better with equal sized kites. If you do decide to stack different sizes, put the smallest kite at the front (nearest the flyer) for the best performance.

There are two main reasons for wanting to stack kites, especially power kites and especially Flexifoils. The first reason is that by adding to the first kite you are increasing the pull on the end of your lines and hence the range of things you can do with the resulting traction. There's a rough formula for working out by how much you increase pull, assuming you're using same-sized kites. When you add a second kite you virtually double the pull. Adding a third adds half as much pull as the first two. A fourth will add about a third of that, and so on. The point is that the pull increases to the extent that, should you decide for some reason that you want to fly a stack of 208 Stacker 6s, as Flexifoil did at the Le Touquet kite festival in 1993, you'll need three bulldozers to anchor the stack and three people heaving on each line to turn it round in the sky.

One advantage of stacking is that a few

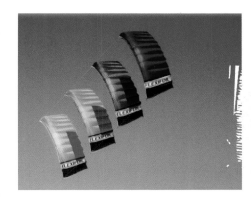

mates with one kite each can get together and have some serious traction going. You'll need friends anyway because when you're flying big stacks in a decent wind you soon get tired and you can pass the stack on to someone else while you laugh at them being dragged all over the spot.

Power kite pull is almost impossible to quantify in terms of things like pounds per square inch or bar, especially with the wind being such a variable factor. What is relatively clear is that you can roughly gauge how the kites pull in relation to each other, even in stacks. Roughly speaking, two Stackers are equal to one Proteam and three Stackers to one Super 10. Two Proteams are equivalent to four Stackers and three Proteams to two Super 10s. Three Super 10s are equivalent to a big nine stack of Stacker 6s.

The second main reason for stacking is aesthetic : it looks brilliant, and that goes for the flyer and anyone else watching. With half a dozen kites stacked you've got a colourful, impressive sky-filler sweeping majestically around the sky. Looking at your kites, feeling the pull and power and knowing that you are in control is an immensely satisfying experience, especially if you know that at any moment you could switch that power to max. for some extremely radical fun.

Follow the instructions for stacking kites together that are included in your Flexifoil instruction manual. There are two different methods suggested. Accurate measuring of your stacking lines and distances is all important as any slight differences in

◄ Stacks look great and are even better to fly
You can stack kites of similar size like these Stacker 6s...
► ...or different sizes like this 6/8/10 stack

stacking lengths will result in the stack not flying correctly, if at all. There's a formula for the correct distance between stacked kites, roughly two-thirds of the length of the leading edge. So, for example, for two Stackers you would need about 4' stacking lines. Flexifoil makes it easy to build up your stack, selling 'add-on' kites, minus the control lines and straps but including a ready-made stacking line kit, which requires nothing more complicated than lark's head knots to attach.

With additional kites attached you're ready to launch your stack. This too can be done solo or assisted. For the solo launch you should use method one for solo launching a single kite, laying the kites right way up at an angle to the wind and pulling them round gently with the flying lines when you're ready to launch. The kites normally inflate and lift off themselves but you may need to take some smooth, steady steps back to get them up. Again, you'll find this easier on a hard sand beach, where there's little to snag the kites

◀ Dig your heels in, lean back and go!

and lines, than on a grassy surface. Don't jerk with your arms and don't persist in dragging the kites if they don't launch.

For an assisted launch your helper should hold the rear kite of the stack, holding it above his head by the spar in the usual way. Once all the kites in the stack are inflated, launch as smoothly as possible, flying the rear kite out of the helper's hand.

Once in flight the stack should, if all your setting up and measuring is correct, 'lock' into position. If it doesn't and the kites are always 'shuffling' or simply not flying there are a few things you can check:

■ Make sure all the kites are attached the right way up.

■ Check that the stacking lines or loops are measured accurately.

■ Adjust the attachment points of a kite that seems to be lagging back, as you would for a single kite with flapping wingtips.

■ Try moving a problem kite to a different position in the stack or swapping its spar with another kite.

Whichever way you decide to build your stack you will need to check your stacking lines (and indeed your flying lines) regularly for wear and tear. The force and friction generated is considerable. Replace any that are worn or damaged straight away.

When the stack is flying smoothly you will immediately feel the extra power and notice that the stack flies slower than a single kite: the more kites you add, the slower it flies. And the stronger it pulls. It's very important that you are aware of the strength and maximum load of your flying lines. The recommended strength for a single kite will normally be sufficient for a stack of two kites the same size. Any more than that and you will need to get some stronger lines or risk a line breaking just when you didn't want it, heavily powered up and getting into a skid or jump. The extra lifting power of the stack will more than compensate for any extra weight of the lines. Consult your local dealer or Flexifoil International who will be happy to advise you. With a decent stack up, you're ready for some more serious power kite action. For starters, how about a bit of skidding and getting some airs, the notorious 'kite jumping'?

SKIDDING

Skidding and body dragging are the first way most people 'discover' the hidden joys of power kiting. Even if eventually you're heading for a kiteboard and the wide blue yonder, you've got to learn how to fly kites and you're going to learn skidding as part of your basic training. Skidding and jumping require even more flying space so make sure you've got plenty of room downwind of where you're flying to allow for your forward movement.

The general idea is to generate enough consistent pull from the stack to pull you

▶ Skidding helps you learn traction basics

along, usually on your feet or on your back, although you can try body surfing in shallow water on your front. You'll be aware that if you keep flying big figure eights with your kite(s) they gain and lose power in relation to their position in the wind window. What you'll need to do to go skidding any distance is keep the kites powered up for long enough to move you along. Here's how it goes.

■ Steer the kites up the centre of the wind window and begin a right hand loop. You can try it in the opposite direction by substituting left for right if you like.

■ As the kites come round their loop towards the centre of the wind window they will begin to seriously power up. Get your feet flat on the ground and lean back to resist being pulled over on your front. You should feel yourself starting to move forward.

■ Keep your shoulders back and your body in a straight line if possible, leaning backwards,

knees slightly bent, shoulders behind hips behind feet. As the kite hits centre window about halfway up pull it into a tighter loop to keep it turning in the centre window thereby keeping it fully powered up. Too tight a spin will lose power so you may need a few goes practice to get it just right. Keep your body position and try to go with the kite, releasing the grip of your feet slightly until you're accelerating forwards.

■ After a few turns you may need to reverse the direction of the kite to untwist your lines but you'll want to keep the power on. Keep the kites roughly in centre window and keep leaning back and sliding forward on the flats of your feet or back.

■ You can 'switch the power off' at almost any time by flying the kites upwards, out of centre window (or out to one edge). Fly the kites up to the park position, stand up and walk back to your start point to have another go.

"The first jumps I started doing were a real buzz, as with most people the first wasn't intentional! A little bit of knowledge is dangerous and you keep pushing things until Mother Nature kicks you up the arse."

Andreya Wharry, Flexifoil team kiteboarder,
Extreme Academy power kite instructor

If you want to try body dragging in water, there's a slightly different technique you can use, which is explained later in the book in the 'Let's get moving' section.

Beaches are great for skidding: hard, flat sand for speed, soft sand for really digging the feet in and 'skiing' along. Inland sites are OK, too, but you'll have a bumpier ride. From personal experience I can thoroughly recommend a grassy playing field, recent rain and plastic waterproof trousers for one of the fastest skids you can get. Make sure you're properly kitted-out wherever you're going to fly. Decent ankle-supporting footwear, sweat shirt and pants to prevent scratching and grazing on the ground, and even a crash helmet, wrist guards and knee pads, may be necessary depending on the conditions and the size of your stack.

KITE JUMPING AND GETTING AIRS

"Many people don't realise how much power the wind can generate and that the weather can change very fast at any time. Whenever you decide to jump with kites, always put safety first. Then get ready for the big adrenaline rush of being 20 feet up in the air with just a kite lifting you across the beach."

Mike Shaw, Flexifoil International sales manager and power kite fanatic

◄ Not recommended, kite jumping
▶ The pendulum effect, swing your feet forwards again for landing

Otherwise known as kite jumping or moon-walking, getting airs is where power kiting really departs from normal ground-based kiting and turns into an exercise in anti-gravity and weightlessness. You may have seen other people getting air born, down at your local beach or flying field or on some power kiting or extreme sport vid down at your local store. You may well have experienced kite jumping inadvertently during your flying and skidding stage, but either way there's probably going to come a time when you want to see what it's like to get air born kite-style. **Kitejumping is not recommended**, even by power kite manufacturers, certainly not by us. But we do recognise that boys will be boys (and girls, girls)…

The first thing to say is that you cannot use kites to fly in the same way as a parachute or paraglider (i.e. jumping off a high object) so please don't try. Nevertheless, you're raising the danger stakes so now you really are going to have to think about some personal protection. The boots, helmets and pads are much more necessary. There are many kite jumping scare stories of jumpers picking up a secondary gust once up in the air, ending up in a vastly different jump situation than the one they'd envisaged a few seconds before. Kite jumping can be a real ankle and wrist

snapper with all those heavy landings. Expect the unexpected and, above all, show proper respect for what you're doing. Even small jumps need big power and if things go wrong under those circumstances you could end up in serious difficulty.

When you're kite jumping, what you're looking for is lift rather than lateral pull. In fact a basic maxim is to concentrate on getting altitude and the wind speed will take care of distance. This means you mustn't bring the kites too low down in the wind window or you'll get too much lateral pull and simply end up going for a facial scrape down the field. The kites must stay higher in the window, which means you never use their full power. That's why you need a lot more sail area up in the sky to get you airborne and that's why it becomes that bit more dangerous.

The ideal kite for jumping will have fast acceleration to haul you up in the air and will be a two line kite to reduce it's manoeuvrability. If you use a four line kite (see Quad-Line power kites page 55) you will need to be very careful as their extra manoeuvrability and strong acceleration are harder to control because of the brake line effect. Stacks of faster-moving two line Flexis or single large two line traction kites specifically designed for jumping are the best option. Whichever you use you will be dealing with a huge amount of kite power.

As you prepare for the jump you will need to resist the kites' pull for as long as possible

◀ Dune jumping, extra height and a soft landing

until the moment of release, levering against them as the power builds up for the jump, then springboarding yourself up with the kites. On a beach you can even dig a hole to give you a wall to lever against. When the moment comes and you let go for your jump, everything happens very quickly and there's a lot of energy involved, your own and the kites'. Jumping with five Super 10s in a 20mph wind means there's about 3 Gs of force on your body as you leave the ground. You're going to need to be reasonably fit and not easily breakable. It's probably not a good idea to start off at that level. Start small and work your way up. It won't be long before you're counting the seconds of flight and measuring your jumps in tens of metres. Discretion is very much the part of valour in power kiting, however, and you shouldn't be embarrassed about stopping if conditions and the size or height of the jumps get too much. Alcohol's not the only thing where one too many can have fatal consequences.

■ Steer the kite(s) up to the park position at the top centre or zenith of the wind window. Get ready to brace your body and find a good 'lever' position. Without pulling the kites into a full loop, steer them across and down one edge of the wind window until they're about half way up (or down) the wind window pointing slightly towards the edge. This is done with a slight pull on either the right or left line. It's common to feel more confident setting a jump up from one side than the other so try both and see which feels best.

How to jump

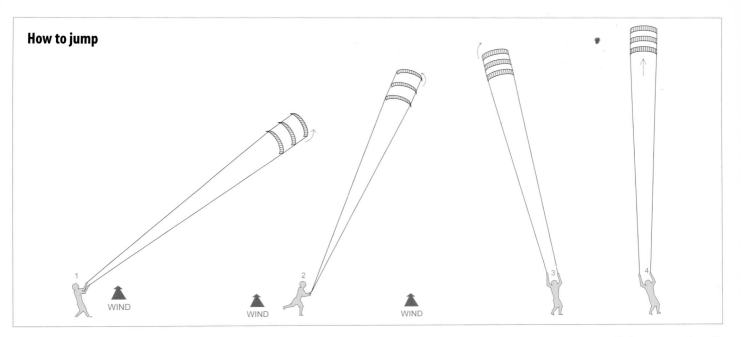

- Now pull slightly with the opposite hand to point the kites in towards the window centre. They will accelerate and pick up power very quickly. Keep leaning back and levering with your body.

- As the kites approach centre window, roughly halfway up, steer them so they fly straight up the wind window. At the same time you can release your resistance to the kite and will feel yourself pulled, jerked off the ground arms first, up into the sky, legs trailing behind you. Hold on tight and enjoy the weightless moment.

- Watch the ground as it rushes up to meet you for touch down and swing your feet and legs forward pendulum style so you can land on your feet or back.

- Once you've hit the ground again you can recover control of the kites. They should be flying up near the top of the wind window with little pull. Pick yourself up and, keeping the kites up at the zenith, you can go back for another go.

There's another way of generating lift that doesn't require levering against the kites' pull, one you can use in lighter winds. As you bring the kites across the window to initiate the jump, run in the opposite direction from the kites' direction of travel, remembering to steer the kites up the window at the appropriate moment. This helps boost the power and leverage to whip you up into the air as the kites power up and drive up the wind window.

Make sure you're really confident before you try and hit any really big airs and you'll have more control over your jumps and avoid accidents. Beaches are a better jump location, especially if there is soft sand, for obvious softer landing reasons. If you feel that it's all getting a bit too big or you pick up one of those second surges from a gust of wind, the best advice is not to let go, hang onto your wrist straps and wait for the kites to bring you down again rather than free-falling. this will largely de-power the kites and give you a hard landing but still with some 'cushioning' by the kites. The only circumstances in which this does not apply are when the kites are dragging or flying you towards a fixed obstacle.

FOUR LINE

"Power Kiting really took off with the introduction of soft, ram air four line kites. These easy-to-use high performance kite engines gave everyone a chance to get into kite traction sports on land, snow or water.

RAY MERRY, PIONEER QUAD LINE DESIGNER, ORIGINAL FLEXIFOIL CO-DESIGNER

As power kiting adapted through the 1990s and all manner of new traction activities had started using kites for power (buggies, landboards, kiteboards, skis…), so the performance requirements for power kites changed enormously too. Though good enough to kick the whole buggy and board thing off, two line power kites like the classic Flexifoil weren't specifically designed for that job and were quite a piloting challenge as a result. The sports fitted themselves around what equipment was available rather than the other way round. No big surprise then that designers put a clean sheet of paper on the drawing board when the time came to address these new power kiting disciplines properly. Responding to a new set of demands, Flexifoil and the steadily growing band of other power kite manufacturers made a giant evolutionary leap forwards, with an entirely new concept for soft, frameless traction kites based on one particular idea: the quad-line concept.

Soft, two line, ram air power kites such as the Peter Lynn 'Peel' range already existed. Soft foils were generally slower moving than Flexifoils but could be made in big enough sizes to deliver the necessary 'grunt' for buggying without the need for stacking. It was clear too from paraglider and parachute design that this type of wing could deliver big power, but it needed the quantum leap of quad line technology to control that power and facilitate the rapid expansion of

appeal in traction kiting. Two simple lengths of flying line made all the difference, the trick was in understanding how to use them…

During the late 1980s, the American kite manufacturer, Revolution, developed its synonymous and revolutionary carbon fibreframed, four line sport kite, the Revolution #1. Instead of two control lines the new kite had four, two each attached to the left and right sides of the kite sail, one at the top and one at the bottom. Special, curved independent control handles were required with two attachment points on each, one handle controlling each side of the kite. Whereas a two line manoeuvrable kite has it's angle of attack (the angle of the sail against the wind) fixed by the bridle lines to move the kite forwards all the time, with the new concept it was possible to engage forward movement by applying pressure to the front (top) lines, then apply pressure to the rear (bottom) ones, thereby altering the angle of attack, slow the kite, stop it and move it in reverse…

It was the kite's ultra-precise manoeuvrability combined with its ability to stand still that caught the imagination. Eagle-eyed traction kite designers, including original Flexifoil codesigner Ray Merry, quickly saw the possibilities and adapted the principle, developing four line soft traction foils which could be 'locked' in position in the sky. It was an enormous success and marked the point at which the numbers of people getting into power kites reached critical mass and the market started to become self-promoting and sustaining.

It works like this. The multiple bridle lines coming from the ram air kite sail come together to form four attachment points, two each on left and right sides of the sail, one controlling the top (front) and the other the bottom (rear) of the sail. Although this type of multiple bridle is more complex to design and not self-adjusting in flight, with four control lines attached it means that the flyer can control the angle of attack and position of the kite more accurately, using the control handles (some of this accuracy is lost when you fly a quad line kite on a control bar) and so create and use a different kind and quantity of power and lift.

On a quad line kite most of the work in terms of load bearing and steering

control is still done by the front lines. The rear lines are there most of the time to help keep the kite in the right shape and for 'braking' it to hold it in position or reduce power. They are much less used for actually going backwards, other than for re-launching from the otherwise impossible face down position, or for landing the kite after a session. For this reason, generally speaking the front lines are stronger than the rear ones. The two independent control handles are each in the form of a short bar, slightly curved near the top. Top and bottom on left and right sides of the kite connect to the corresponding top and bottom of each handle. There's a small risk of attaching your flying lines upside down or on the wrong side. Nowadays line sets are sold with colour coded sleeved loops so you can tell at a glance which is which. Follow the instructions and take great care when attaching your flying lines. Incorrect attachment can render the kite uncontrollable and dangerous.

The size and efficiency of these traction kites explains the common use of body harnesses, like those used by windsurfers, by serious power kiters. A loop of heavy line connecting the tops of your handles or vinyl strop coming from the rear of your control bar is hooked into the harness. This enables you to carry most of the pull on your legs and body, relieving pressure on your arms. Steering happens as normal with the loop of line sliding through your harness hook or pulley, control

bar loops pivoting around the fixed point. You shouldn't try using a harness until you have fully mastered flying your four line kite without. It doesn't take long to adapt to flying with four lines but as ever, spend some time fully familiarising yourself with flying a smaller kite before you try getting radically powered up.

Although four lines might seem to increase the possibility of line tangles, nowadays all aspects of power kiting are geared to delivering maximum fun with minimum fuss. You shouldn't have problems if you are organised about how you handle your flying lines. In any event they are a critical element of the whole kit and need to be respected as much as the kite itself. Always allow time at the end of your session to pack up in an orderly way and always immobilise your kite properly when not in use. Bad winding and a kite that blows away down the field are two common causes of fouled lines.

Quad line soft foils are not usually flown in stacks; most quad line flyers have a range of kites in different sizes to enable flying in a wide range of winds. In many other respects four line kites are no different, with the same wind window and other physical limits, from their two line predecessors. Just because they're soft don't kid yourself that they can't damage or be damaged. They are susceptible and sensitive to nicks and tears in the fabric from contact with rough ground. Over-stretching can also be a problem, especially if a kite is flown above its recommended wind range for lengthy periods, not uncommon when a serious buggyer or kiteboarder

▲ Four line kite handles with safety leash
◀ A Sabre in flight showing the 'complex' bridle structure

is heavily powered-up going for maximum speed or lift. And a heavy, vent down, fully inflated and powered up landing can easily burst a sail panel, or worse, one of the internal ribs that are critical to the airflow and pressure within the sail. Likewise, with so much power in play, slamming the kite into a bystander could cause them serious injury. Remember, safety is the responsibility of the flyer.

Care taken by the R&D department means that different sized kites of all Flexifoil ram air models have similar, consistent handling, making it easy to adjust to them when changing up or down a size. Flexifoil currently has three complete models of high performance quad line ram air kites, each designed to meet specific needs, responding to and anticipating the diverse and rapidly evolving demands of modern traction kiting. And there's another component of the Flexifoil quad line range, an entry level kite, perfect for beginners just getting to grips with quad line flying, as a trainer for more serious traction kiting, or for competent recreational flyers looking for another kind of flying experience.

QUAD LINE POWER KITES: RAGE, BLADE, SABRE AND STING

Quad line kites have made it possible for more people to enjoy the serious traction kite experience with greater ease, allowing

▶ Flexifoil Sabre: advanced level land and snow kite

themselves to be pulled along and concentrating more on steering the buggy or board, less on piloting the kite. The kites divide into three basic categories : high, medium and low aspect ratio, each of which is appropriate to a particular skill level, performance, activity or all of those. More elongated kites are high aspect ratio and higher performance – better for experienced flyers; shorter wingspan, more oblong or rounded kites are low aspect ratio – better for beginners.

And what better place to start looking at these kites than with the **Sting**, Flexifoil's low aspect ratio, beginner quad line kite. Or should I say four kites, because there are four sizes ranging from 1.2 to 3.3 m^2 and with an aspect ratio between 3 and 3.5, what you'd call low. Low aspect ratio means excellent stability and smooth, consistent turn speed. The Sting is made from Chikara ripstop nylon, the cells across its span are open vented, it's got a deep wing profile and can be flown on independent handles or a control bar according to pilot preference. It's the perfect kite for learning quad line flying, generating light, controllable pull, even in the 3.3 m2 size. The flat trailing edge of its stubby, semi-eliptical shape lends itself well to learning braking and reverse flying and the whole thing packs away into a handy wide-vented stuff bag so that, like the Buzz, you really can take it anywhere. All sizes come with a wrist leash re-ride safety release system for complete ease of mind.

"I wanted to start quad lining with a 4 metre Bullet but was advised that a 3 metre was better adapted to my skill level. A couple of months later I took 2nd place in my first ever buggy race flying my 3 metre; my son came 3rd flying a 2 metre."

Richard Brazier, Flexifoil International kitebuggy driver

The **Rage** is the medium skill level quad line kite in the Flexifoil range. It was developed from their earlier Bullet kite by the Flexifoil R&D team brains to become their medium performance land foil, easy enough to help you learn your traction sport and performing enough to help you progress. It's an ultra-stable aerofoil, medium aspect ratio kite, semi-eliptical in shape to minimise drag and

increase its power-to-size ratio. It has a gauze-covered leading edge vent running the whole span of the kite to help 'inflate' the kite quickly for launch and re-launch, also to keep sand etc. out. The bridle is made from tough, sleeved Dyneema. The Rage is powerful but still easy to handle. It's available in five different sizes, from 1.8 to 6.0 square metres, the larger sizes requiring at least intermediate skill level because, despite their super stable handling, they develop serious amounts of grunt! The Rage is fantastically versatile, a great all-rounder and suitable for various land-based power kite activities: recreational flying, kite landboarding, kitebuggying and snowkiting. What it is not is a 'water' kite. That's to say you

▲ The Sting's flatter, squarer shape makes it super stable

should not, under any circumstances, try to use the Rage for kiteboarding on water. There are other toys in the Flexifoil cupboard much better suited to that kind of thing...

> **"Nothing takes you higher faster than a Blade. It's like a rocket launcher. If you want big airs and high adrenaline get a Blade. It's the most stable high performance foil kite out there making it ideal for all kinds of kite traction sports."**
>
> Mike Shaw, Flexifoil International sales manager and power kite fanatic

Like many of the pioneering kiteboard equipment manufacturers, Flexifoil's first solution to the kite for water or board use was already established as the Formula One model in their ram air foil range when kiteboarding first started, the **Blade**. The high aspect ratio Blade, another Andrew Jones original design, has since become a best-selling power kite legend and is now in its fourth generation of development. The resulting refinements and improvements which designer Luke Rebbeck has included on the latest generation Blade reflect that and make it one of the most sophisticated and performing ram air kites on the market. It has an ellipsoidal outline and rounded wing tips, a well-proven wing form giving a solid structure and good aerodynamic properties across the whole span. It's a kite for intermediate to expert level flyers that develops phenomenal pull and lift. The Blade was originally developed and is excellent for general land use, making it a great kite for advanced level landboarders,

buggyers and snowkiters. It's available in five different sizes from 4.0 to 10.5 square metres. The wing tips have a thinner aerofoil section, improving the kite's turn speed, plus wing tip vents to facilitate emptying of sand, water and snow from inside the kite. Blades were the kites used by Flexifoil's three-man team on their successful first ever Channel crossing by kiteboard in 1999.

The third of Flexifoil's big three serious traction kite models is the **Sabre**, now into its second generation. This kite was specifically designed for what are the latest fast-growing power kite sports, snowkiting and landboarding. Both sports are starting to attract large numbers of newcomers and snowkiting particularly posed a number of new design questions. In fact the Sabre is suitable for all land-based power kite sports but, like the Rage, not intended for water use. It took two years of analysing snowkiting and landboarding and what people doing those sports wanted, to develop the Sabre, and the wait was well worth it. It's an open-vented foil with a very efficient de-power system (more on this in a minute), which gives it superior light wind performance and full launch-land autonomy and safety: when the kite reverse lands it spills its air and de-powers quickly. It's stable in flight but its cross bridle pulley system gives it excellent turn speed in relation to size. It's versatile, available in four sizes from 5 to 12 m², each with a wide wind range thanks to the de-power system, plus excellent safety features (including a self-landing handle, spinning safety leash and two quick releases), both of which are important considerations in snowkiting where, specially in the mountains, conditions can change quickly. It gives smooth power delivery, giving you the confidence to concentrate more on (improving) your riding than on what the kite is doing. The Sabre2 also includes a 5th line, another idea borrowed from water kiteboarding, for full, safe rider autonomy. The 5th line principle, is explained in the water kites chapter on page 123.

The Sting, Rage and Blade can be flown with either control bar on independent handles, whereas the Sabre is for control bar flying only. Different activities may be better suited to different systems so make sure you discuss the options thoroughly with your dealer before purchasing and that they give you what's most appropriate. Using a control bar is enormously different from using independent handles. If you're used to flying your kite on handles and you decide to switch to a control bar, make sure you fully familiarise yourself with the differences in handling of your kite before you try powering up for any serious traction action.

SET UP AND PACK UP PROCEDURES

The Sting comes in a simple stuff bag, but Flexifoil's high performance quad line kites all come in a stronger carry bag, a padded, customised backpack bag with sand and

▶ Four line kites have made buggying much simpler

moisture vent and control gear storage (it holds your handles and/or bar as well as the kite). This enables you to access difficult spots carrying your kite, and to carry a spare kite on your back when riding, giving you somewhere to temporarily pack up the one you're using if you have to change kite sizes. Try unpacking and re-packing your kite indoors once at least to familiarise yourself with the process, rather than going straight out to the flying field. The kites come with appropriate strength flying lines, which, in the case of the Sting, are pre attached to the kite bridles. For serious traction activities where resistance is much greater, such as kiteboarding, or for flying in very strong winds, you may need to upgrade these, in which case consult your dealer.

Follow the step-by-step manufacturer's instructions for setting up and packing up your kites. In the unlikely event that you have a problem, take the kite back to your local dealer for advice, or contact Flexifoil direct, their details are given at the end of the book. Try to remember how the kite was packed when you first unfold it and try to always re-pack it the same way. See also the care and maintenance of your equipment section of the book for other recommended storage and packing tips. Your instruction manual also covers setting up your flying lines and attaching your control handles or control bar. Flexifoil quad line kites come with 25 metre flying line sets. You will need to attach the

lines to the kite and your control gear when you set up for the first time. Thereafter, you can leave everything permanently attached if you wish. Flexifoil quad line sets are colour coded to avoid mistakes when attaching flying lines. Check and double check that you have correctly attached them. You will need to be familiar with the lark's head knot to correctly attach your flying lines to the kite and/or control gear, so if you skipped that bit of the earlier section covering recreational Flexifoil kites it's time to go back and check it out now.

Whether you fly them using handles or control bar, Flexifoil quad line kites come fitted with a safety wrist leash, which you should use at all times. The Sabre's safety leash can also be attached to the de-power loop you hook into your control bar for flying, but means that you have to ride hooked in to be able to benefit from it. Whichever you have, the system is quite straightforward to use, a simple cord coming from the handles or bar attached to your wrist by a velcro strap. The leash is attached to the brake or rear lines. Using handles you will have one safety leash for each handle or wrist. Using a control bar there is just one leash, either running through an eyelet on the control bar centre, or, in the case of the Sabre, passing under the control bar to attach to the rear lines at the point where they join the leader lines. It's up to you which wrist you attach the leash to. The safety system can be actioned anytime you feel that the situation you're in or getting into is too much for you to deal with, the classic being over-powered and going too fast for comfort.

◀ Flexifoil Blade, market leader for almost a decade

If all other attempts to control the kite fail, you unhook (if you're hooked into your harness) and let go of the handles or bar. The leash pulls on the brake lines of your kite but the front lines are released, spilling all air virtually instantaneously from the kite, de-powering it almost completely and bringing it harmlessly back down to land or water. It's easy then to recover the controls and re-launch your kite. Always test your safety system so that you and it are fully prepared for when you need to use it for real. The safety leash is there for your and for other site users' safety, make sure you know how to use it.

So, having fastened your velcro straps to set up the safety leash, make sure your open space is still free of other people and obstacles and check that the wind hasn't changed direction; it can be very shifty at times, especially inland. It's recommended that you make your first few flights in light to moderate wind until you get used to how the kite handles and pulls. If it's all looking good at this point, you're ready to fly.

HOW TO LAUNCH, FLY AND LAND USING INDEPENDENT HANDLES

Launching the kite

Under normal circumstances you should be able to solo launch. Launch-land autonomy is normally one of the advantages ram air kites have over inflatable tube kites, specially

▶ Kite landboarding flying with a control bar

when flown on independent handles. Pick up the handles, take one handle in each hand holding it firmly by the foam cushioned section at the top, curve away from you and the bottom of the handles further towards the kite than the top. The front flying line leaders should come out from between your index and second fingers. This is the 'neutral' position for normal flight. Make a last minute check that your lines are connected correctly and untwisted and that you have clear space in front. The wind should be on your back with you and the kite in centre window. The kite should still be on its back, the trailing edge weighted down to immobilise it.

- Pull back gently and steadily with both handles keeping equal pressure on all four lines. The front or leading edge will lift up and the kite will begin to inflate with air pressure. As it inflates the kite will stand up on its trailing edge ready to take off. You can hold it steady at this point by pushing forward slightly with the top of both handles until you're ready for launch

- Pull sharply on all four lines, bringing your hands (thumbs leading) back towards your shoulders, to fully inflate the kite and it will start to lift off. Keep slightly more pressure on the front lines. You may need to take a few steps back to get it moving depending on the wind conditions. The kite will fly straight up the wind window as long as you pull evenly on all four lines, through the power zone, to come to a rest with minimum power in the 'park' position at the top centre or zenith of the window. Be ready to deal with the

pull as the kite hits the power zone, leaning back and ready to move forwards a little on the ground. You will need to 'play' the handles slightly (find the correct balance point between front and rear lines) to stabilise or park the kite. Be careful, don't over-do it or the kite may react suddenly…

Let's take a quick look at the other solo launch method and assisted launching for the high performance quad line kites. Both are for use in strong winds, when it's inadvisable to launch in centre window as the kite will hit the strongest power zone of the window immediately after

▲ Left: The correct grip and 'neutral' position for independent handles, safety leashes attached

▲ Right: Launch your kite by pulling back mostly with the top lines

launch and can be very dangerous for you and other people if it pulls you forwards suddenly. You need to set the kite up closer to the edge of the wind window in relation to where you stand at window centre. Lay the kite on its back but this time lengthways downwind so that the wind blows across the kite from tip to tip, leading edge vents facing towards the edge of the window. For solo launching, fold the upwind tip of the kite in once and weight it down with sand or a back pack, leaving the downwind tip free. Next :

■ Pick up your handles and pull gently on the downwind end of the kite (the tip furthest away), which will lift the tip and leading edge enough to allow the kite to inflate. Keep even pressure on the two lines on the downwind tip handle.

■ Keep pulling steadily with the downwind handle until your hands are parallel, then pull steadily with both and the kite will launch and fly itself towards the edge of the wind window. Keep slightly more line pressure on the front lines as the kite lifts off.

■ Keep pulling slightly on the downwind handle (connected to the upper tip of the kite as you see it) and steer the kite carefully up the edge of the wind window to the zenith where you can neutralise your steering and get ready for action.

If using an assisted launch, first of all make sure your helper understands what to do. To launch a Sting, use the same system as described earlier for the Buzz, remembering to move the kite away from the maximum power area (centre window) towards the window edge in strong winds.

Assisted launch for the high performance quad lines is done slightly differently.

- Your helper should stand towards the edge of the window, behind the kite, holding it by the back of the sail and leading edge so that the leading edge is facing the wind, pointing towards the edge of the wind window.

- Once the kite is inflated and you're ready, signal to the helper to release the kite. This means simply letting it go rather than trying to throw the kite into the sky, which will actually prevent a smooth take off.

- As they release, you fly the kite out of their hands pulling slightly on the upper tip to steer the kite up the edge of the wind window to the zenith.

FLYING AND STEERING THE KITE

You can hold the kite at the zenith for as long as you like but as soon as you're ready you should start with some basic turns. To begin with, keep the kite high in the wind window and make gentle control movements. This will keep it out of the extreme pull of the power zone while you get used to the handling. The basic turn manoeuvre is similar to a dual line kite.

- When the kite is climbing up the middle of the wind window and is nearing the

▲ Solo launch
▶ Assisted launch

zenith, pull back on the right handle keeping tension on both lines. The kite turns to the right and starts making a wide, full loop in that direction.

- Keep the same amount of pull on the right handle until the kite has flown a complete circle and is climbing up the wind window again, pointing straight up.

- Bring your handles back to the neutral position with more tension on the front control lines and the kite flies straight up.

- Now pull on the left handle to execute a left loop and uncross your flying lines.

You will find that as much as you pull with one handle you push with the other because of the angle of your body and this in fact makes the smoothest turn. Keeping even tension on all four lines most of the time will give you a feeling similar to flying a two line kite. But once you've understood how the kite handles you can also start to make different, tighter turns by using the extra control possibilities of the two extra lines.

- As you begin a loop, whichever handle is being pulled should be pivoted so that the rear line is pulled as well as the top. To do this, pivot your wrist pushing your thumb away from you and pointing the top of the handle more towards the kite. The kite will turn faster, even spin on its axis. You may feel a slight reduction of pull during a tight turn like this.

- As the kite comes round full circle bring the handles back to the neutral position with both thumbs back to resume normal flying and feel the power 'switch' back on.

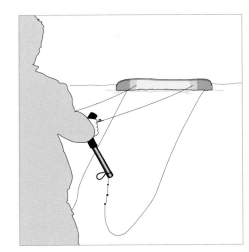

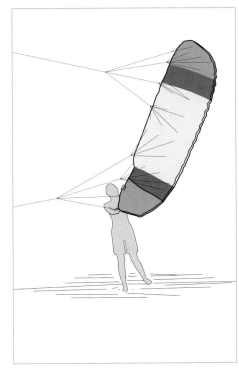

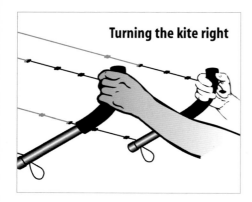

Turning the kite right

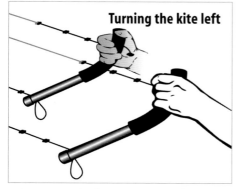

Turning the kite left

It may need a few goes to get the timing right but with practice you will be able to accelerate through and out of the turn with minimal – if any – power loss.

As your flying becomes more confident you can experiment with more power. Flying alternate left and right loops in a kind of flat figure eight in the centre of the wind window will give the best and most consistent pull as a fixed flyer (as opposed to one moving on a board or buggy etc.) and stop the lines twisting too much.

Four line control with handles means

having the ability to stop and reverse the kite, even de-power it if needed. It requires a lot of wrist action and brings the rear lines fully into play. You stop and reverse the kite by changing the aerodynamics in such a way that the trailing edge becomes the leading edge.

- With the kite flying up the middle of the window, leading edge pointing straight up, rotate both handles gently by pointing your thumbs forward until the kite 'brakes'. You should see a 'crease' line appear across the kite sail close to the trailing edge.

- Keep pulling on the rear lines and the kite slows to a stop. Practise this manoeuvre, stopping the kite and holding it steady, as that's how you will be able to really use the power – 'locking' the kite in position – when the time comes to get moving (see next chapter).

- Now slowly engage more rear line pressure, evenly on both sides, and the kite starts to reverse. Don't overdo it or the kite may 'stall'. When this happens the rear or trailing edge of the kite folds in on itself. If this happens pull sharply on the front lines to move the kite forwards again, unfolding the folded trailing edge, then gradually engage backwards flight as before – this time more gently.

- To resume normal flying, rotate the handles back to the neutral position by bringing your thumbs towards you again and pull on the front lines.

With experience you'll be able to control the rear lines much better, reversing your kite from the top of the window all the way

to the ground. Fine adjustments of your braking and 'playing' the handles (making small, fine adjustments to line tensions) a little will enable you to position and hold the kite just where you want it almost anywhere in the window. Practice braking and stopping the kite in a vertical (one tip up, one tip down) and diagonal axis as this is how you will need to position the kite when it comes to getting moving on a board or buggy. When holding the kite vertically you will need to position your hands similarly, one above the other, handles held almost horizontally.

LANDING THE KITE

Once you master stopping and reversing the kite you'll be able to land it easily, when and where you want, conditions permitting (in strong wind you'll have to land near the edge of the window). Technically speaking it can be done anywhere in the wind window as long as the leading edge is pointing up. In practice you may find that it's easier to begin with trying it nearer to the edge of the wind window where there's less power in the sail. And the bigger your kite the more power there will be to compensate for. Be careful though, too close to the edge could make the kite unstable and require some juggling to keep it steady.

- With the kite pointing straight up, as close to the ground as you can, and your handles in the neutral position, apply almost full brakes by rotating both wrists so the top of the handles are pointing at the kite. You should be flying on virtually the brake lines only. The kite slows and stops very quickly, de-powering it.

■ Keep the rear lines on full. The kite will descend backwards to the ground and settle on its trailing edge. Don't try to go too fast backwards or it may 'flip out', bottom towards you. You may well need to 'play' the handles quite a lot coming down the last few metres to keep the kite steady.

It will take a bit of practice to get right but once you've landed it's up to you whether you want to re-launch or stop flying. You should be able to reverse the kite from the zenith to the ground. To immobilise the kite, peg or weight down the handles on the ground by the loops at the bottom, keeping tension on the rear lines as you do so. Then go and weight the trailing edge of the kite down.

There's another solo landing technique you can try, for use in stronger winds when it becomes too difficult to reverse land. It's very simple and uses the neutralising effect of the safety leashes.

■ Fly the kite out towards the minimum power area near the edge of the wind window, bringing the kite low near the ground.

■ When the kite nears the edge of the window, let go of both handles. The kite is retained by its brake lines, de-powers instantly and sinks to the ground. Stake down the loops on the brake line or hold the handles in maximum brake position while you or your helper

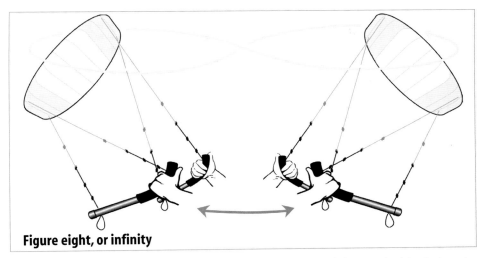

Figure eight, or infinity

weights the kite down with sand or a back pack to immobilise it.

In a very strong wind you will find it very difficult to land the kite, let alone immobilise it before it blows away. It's often better to ask someone to help you land, as they may have done for the launch.

■ Position your helper at one edge of the wind window and your kite at the zenith.

■ Pull slightly on the tip nearest to your helper, pulling with even pressure on both lines. The kite should slowly make its way down the curved edge of the wind window towards the ground, finishing in vertical position, leading edge pointing towards the window edge.

■ As it reaches touching distance of your helper, steady the kite as much as possible. Your helper should grab the kite from behind by the lower tip and immediately weight the tip down with sand

or a back pack, letting the kite lie lengthways downwind.

RE-LAUNCHING AND RECOVERING THE KITE

Another advantage of four line flying is that you can re-launch from almost any position. Generally you'll find that the kite is either on its trailing edge, in which case re-launch is obvious, or its leading edge (going forwards into the ground, making re-launch a little less obvious). But if you can reverse the kite in the sky it logically follows that you can reverse it off the ground, too: what's known as reverse launching.

■ With the kite on the ground, fully inflated and standing on its leading edge, pull backwards (it may need you to walk backwards a few steps too) with the rear lines fully engaged. The kite should begin to rise

backwards of the ground. You will often need to 'play' the handles to keep it going steadily.

- Keep pulling back on the rear lines and, as the kite rises, push one of the rear lines forward by pivoting the handle. This engages one of the front lines, causing the kite to pivot, but be aware that with the kite pointing downwards, if you pull on the front right line it's the left tip of the kite as you see it that will respond. It's easier to turn the kite up and away from window centre rather than down towards it, as the kite will tend to accelerate towards centre window and into the ground.

- When it's pointing straight up the window you can fly away by pulling evenly on both handles.

▲ Serious snowkiting with a Flexifoil Sabre

If that doesn't work there's another recovery you can try. It involves turning the kite onto its trailing edge so the leading edge is pointing straight up, then you can re-launch in the normal way. This is normally easiest if you try to 'roll' it over **towards** the window centre. If the kite is directly downwind of you, walk a few paces to one side to create a new centre window, which will automatically create a new position for the kite, closer to the edge of the window.

- Pull back on one handle only, the one connected to the side of the kite furthest from window centre, the bottom of the handle more than the top. The tip of the kite will lift up and rise until the kite is standing vertically, leading edge pointing out of the wind window.

- At this point you can start bringing the handle you already pulled slowly back to the neutral position, still with more pressure on the bottom line. The kite should continue to roll down to a horizontal position, leading edge pointing up.

- As the kite reaches the correct position use your rear lines to keep it still on the ground while you get ready to launch in the normal way.

TROUBLESHOOTING

Under normal circumstances nothing should go wrong but if for any reason the kite doesn't perform as expected there are a few things you can check :

- The bridles are not twisted.

- The flying lines are correctly attached, heaviest lines on the front, left lines to left handle etc.

- You've got the handles in the correct hands.

- That one or all the lines haven't stretched. In fact, stretching can occur during your first few sessions, until the lines are fully 'flown in'. Check your lines regularly to make sure they are still all the same length. What to do about this is explained in the 'Care of the kite' chapter at the end of the book.

If the kite is sluggish on take off and slow through the sky the chances are that your brake lines are too short or the main lines are too long. If the kite is unresponsive to steering and difficult to reverse check that either the brake lines are too long or the main lines too short. In either of the above scenarios you can make an adjustment at the handles, shortening or lengthening as appropriate, using the leader line knots. If there is only one knot – on the end of the leader line – you can add one or two more by tying thumb knots at regular spaces along the rest of the leader line. In fact these leader line options can be used to tune your kite to suit your riding style. For heavier pull and tighter turns shorten your brake lines or lengthen your front lines. For lighter pull and slower, wider turns lengthen your brake lines or shorten your front lines. If the tips or trailing edge of the kite are flapping there may be sand inside it. Land and empty the sand out through the vents at the front (or wind tip vents on a Blade).

If the kite still won't fly, contact your dealer

or Flexifoil International direct. If the kite's flying as it should you can expect to learn very quickly. Talk to other, more experienced flyers if you can. Their advice can save you an awful lot of learning-from-your-mistakes time. After a few sessions you should be a competent quad line kite flyer and ready for some more serious action. Before deciding which way you want to get moving, there's something else you should consider.

FLYING QUAD LINE KITES ON A CONTROL BAR

Some of the more recent additions to the list of power kite sports, board sports in particular, are better suited to flying the kites using a control bar rather than independent handles. There are advantages and disadvantages to both, much as you'd expect. For board (and ski) riders, control bars work because they give you something more solid to use to lock your body in position against while giving enough freedom of movement to be able to move the bar to steer. Not only that, a control bar makes a much better 'trapeze' for aerial gymnastics and it reduces the sensitivity of the kite's response, the kite stays in position during jumps. Also, for the very good reason that you can fit a de-power system to a control bar, whereas with handles it's how you fly the kite that is your only de-power.

Flying quad line on a control bar doesn't, however, give you the full mobility of independent handles so you won't have the same

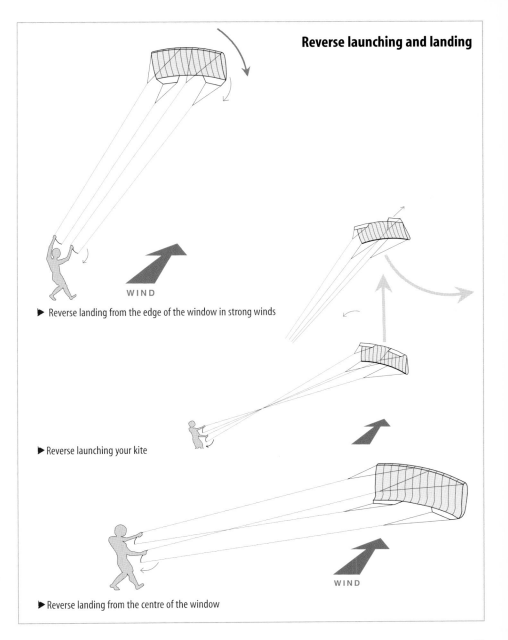

Reverse launching and landing

▶ Reverse landing from the edge of the window in strong winds

▶ Reverse launching your kite

▶ Reverse landing from the centre of the window

WIND

WIND

control for reverse landing for example. The rear control lines are connected (via their single leader line) to the centre of the bar and have little influence on steering. The front lines are connected to the wing tip leader lines and control most of the steering. Without the ability to pivot the controls to change the kite's angle of attack you can't lock or reverse your kite in the same way. Where board sports are generally easier using a control bar, buggying is arguably easier with independent handles because, with your body movement much more limited (sitting down) you can't get enough independent movement of your hands using a bar. 'Arguably', because there are plenty of people out there buggying on control bars disproving the rule.

QUICK RELEASE SAFETY SYSTEMS

All the control bars have their built in wrist leash safety system, which we've already described. In the event of getting into unrecoverable difficulty you can simply let go of the control bar. It will slide up as far as a stop on the rear lines keeping those taught, allowing the front lines to extend and the kite sail to de-power itself, drifting harmlessly back to the ground and allowing you to recover it safely and with no bother.

That's great if you're riding without a har-

◀ Four line flying with a harness: note the harness strop linking the tops of each handle via the pilot's harness hook

ness, or not hooked into your harness, but what can you do if you are hooked in ? It's no good just letting go of the bar, it's attached to your harness. And the kite may well be pulling too hard for you to unhook. There's a primary additional safety system on the harness loop, at the point where it joins the control bar. It's a strap-to-strap quick release, similar to the one on the AXIS bar used for flying water kites, which makes it efficient to use and simple to re-set. The release itself takes the form of a plastic tube, fluted towards the end nearest the control bar. To action the quick release you grab the tube and push it away from you, pushing against the fluted end of the tube. Your control bar will be instantaneously released and the kite retained by your wrist leash attached to one of the rear brake lines. With all front line tension gone the kite spills all its air and falls back to the ground. Once the kite has landed, you can recover the control bar by pulling on the leash, re-set your quick release and recover the kite. Practise releasing and, more importantly, re-setting your quick release before you need to use it in an emergency, so that it becomes instinctive. If in any doubt, particularly about re-setting, consult your dealer or Flexifoil direct. An incorrectly set quick release could be dangerous.

If, for any reason, you find that the released kite is still impossible to control or recover, putting you in further danger, you can as a last resort let go of the whole rig by grabbing and ripping open the Velcro wrist fastening (different for the Sabre, see below). This should only be done as a final solution:

a released kite will blow away downwind, presenting a potential risk to other site users and you with some considerable chasing and sorting out to do afterwards. Make sure you practise your safety drills thoroughly in moderate conditions so that if you ever need to use them for real they will be instinct rather than guesswork.

The Sabre has two additional levels of safety mechanism: quick releases built into the control gear, allowing you to instantly kill the power, neutralise the kite, and – in the final case – totally separate yourself from it. As before, if you're flying unhooked (from your harness) your first option is to let go of the control bar and let the safety leash retain the rear lines to 'kill' the kite. This is a re-ride system, it's easy to recover the bar and re-launch. If, on the other hand, you're flying or riding hooked in, letting go of the bar won't kill the kite, simply de-power it slightly to the point where the bar locks against the de-power stop. If you haven't got time to unhook and let go of the bar or it's not possible because the kite's pulling too much, grab the primary release toggle (a red plastic ball located between your chicken loop and the front lines leader line) and pull it firmly towards you. Once activated, the system completely releases the front lines leader line, retaining the kite by the rear lines and your chicken loop. Where the safety leash attaches to your wrist or chicken loop there's a second red plastic ball, the secondary release system. Pushing this toggle away from your wrist or chicken loop activates it, but be careful, this totally detaches you from your kite,

which will escape and present a possible danger to other site users. It's the ultimate solution for your personal safety but should only be used as a genuine last ditch option. The primary and secondary release systems are **not** re-ride; you'll have to stop and re-set the safety releases before you can continue your session. Follow the clear instructions for re-setting and if in any doubt consult your dealer or Flexifoil direct. Test it to make sure you understand correct re-setting. A badly re-set safety release may not function correctly, putting you at risk.

LAUNCHING THE KITE

Whichever kite you're flying, make sure you attach the lines / control bar as described in your instruction manual. Check that the lines are correctly connected and untwisted, and get your body in position ready to launch.

In lighter winds it's really very simple, you can solo launch from centre window. First, weight the kite trailing edge down. When you're ready to launch, take a few steps backwards holding your control bar, pulling evenly on all four lines. The leading edge of the kite will lift up first enabling the vents to take in wind to inflate the body of the kite. As it lifts up and inflates the kite will power up and launch, dumping whatever you had used for weight from the trailing edge and flying straight up towards the zenith. To solo launch a Sabre, push your bar away towards its maximum de-power position to enable the kite to climb and avoid heavy lateral pull

in the main power area. As an alternative to de-powering you could try holding the bar with one hand, grabbing the 'V' of the front leader lines where they come out of the de-power adjustment and pulling it towards you. This will sheet in the front lines, helping the kite fully inflate faster and launch, at which point you release the front lines. The kite will launch and fly straight up the wind window, coming to a stop at the zenith.

There's a different solo technique for stronger winds and you may actually feel more comfortable asking someone to help you. You can use this assisted launch anytime you like but it's actually recommended you always use it in very strong winds.

■ Launching in stronger winds with a control bar should always be done across the wind, with the kite laid out on the window edge lengthways downwind, with the upwind tip weighted down with sand or dirt. For an assisted launch, your helper should position themselves behind the kite, holding it by the back of the sail with the leading edge pointing to the edge of the wind window.

■ When you're ready, take up the slack on the lines. This will initially lift the downwind tip of the kite, allowing the kite to inflate as wind enters through the vents. For assisted launching, you should wait until the kite is well inflated but still being held.

◀ To-the-limits buggy driving, 100% Flexifoil-equipped

■ Keep pulling (you may need to take a couple of steps back) and when the kite is fully inflated it will lift off and turn itself to face upwind. Signal to your helper to let go in the recommended manner.

■ Steer the kite carefully up the edge of the window to the zenith by pulling gently on the upper tip of the kite with the control bar. Then bring the bar to a 'neutral' position to 'park' the kite there.

STEERING

As before, keep the kite high in the window while you get used to how it handles. Normal turning is done by pulling one side of the bar towards you. A faster turn speed can be obtained by pulling on one side of the bar and pushing with the other, pivoting it around the centre, the same kind of pull–push as you've already tried with independent handles. Pull right to go right, pull left to go left. It will feel different from how the kite flies on handles so take some time to accustom yourself to its handling before you try full power. But it's still the same kite and will perform in the same way as regards how and where in the wind window it pulls, etc. The Sabre's cross bridle pulley system is very responsive to pull–push steering, turning the kite tight and smooth. Practise some figure eight manoeuvres so you fly alternate left and right loops, making sure you can do it well to both sides. Once you've mastered loops to left and right, try some horizontal passes (not too low down) with the kite in a vertical axis. Holding the control bar on an angle or even vertically will help. This is the 'traction' position, one you should be able to lock the kite into when you come to get moving on a board with apparent wind.

Now that you're flying on a control bar you will not have the same facility to slow the kite down, stop or reverse, so, unless you're flying a Sabre (in which case you've got a de-power system – see below), if at any stage you need to lose some power you will need to fly the kite out to the edge of the wind window, either at one side or at the zenith. Likewise, you won't have the same ability to 'lock' the kite in position, at least not while you're 'static' flying. Once you get moving on a board or skis that apparent wind factor we mentioned comes into play, which does enable you to do that more effectively.

THE DE-POWER SYSTEM: APPLIES TO SABRE ONLY

This de-power system has been mentioned enough now so perhaps it's time to explain what it's all about. Especially as it's one of the plus features of the Sabre range. De-power systems were invented as a safety device for inflatable water kites (see Kites for Water) as a means of being able to control and adjust the power delivery from the huge sail areas of those kites. It's more recently that the system has been successfully adapted to ram air kites, using the same principle.

▶ Sabre kite and control bar showing the de-power and safety systems

The first thing to say is that to benefit from the de-power system you need to be flying or riding with your control bar hooked onto your harness by means of the heavy duty loop or strop on the rear of the bar. The loop itself is attached to a single leader line passing through the centre eyelet of the control bar and which forms the attachment point for the two front control lines. That gives you a fixed connection to the front of the kite. Meanwhile, the rear lines are attached to the tips of the bar, not to you. You can now push the control bar away from you, sliding it along the centre line, which will have the effect of pushing the trailing edge of the kite away (sheeting out), spilling wind from the sail and reducing the power. The inverse also applies. If you pull the bar towards you, the trailing edge is pulled (sheeted) in so that the kite becomes flatter against the wind and the power increases. In both cases there is a stop which sets the maximum distance you can move the bar. Beyond the de-power stop (the furthest one away) is an adjustment or trim with a strap which allows you to adjust the overall power tuning for the de-power system, dictating the de-power range. Pulling the strap, further in will shorten the front lines and reduce power, lengthening the strap will lengthen the front lines, increasing power.

There are two obvious benefits to this system. One is that you can power up and down (within a certain range) according to what activity or move you're actually doing. The other is that you've got the ability to absorb gusts, or power up through lulls if you're flying in irregular winds. It helps extend the kite's wind range and reduce the number of different sized kites you might need. You'll need to spend some time adjusting to the different feel the de-power system gives to the kite's handling, not least in one important respect. Whereas up to now, once flying, to get a kite to climb you've had to develop a reflex to pull backwards, now you're going to have to forget all that. Sheeting in or pulling the control bar towards you (assuming you're riding or flying hooked in) will increase the pull but slow the kite down and actually stop it climbing. To help it climb faster you need to get into the new habit of sheeting out / pushing the bar away from you. But doing that alters the angle of attack of the kite, which means de-powering and losing traction. Once you get on a board you'll need to learn how to compensate, how to work your board in synch with the way you work the kite. The benefit of de-power systems is a skill you must learn: that of combining keeping the kite moving where you want, when you want, with generating the power you want.

LANDING

Without the ability to fully reverse land, this too will be done differently. You can self-land all Flexifoil high performance traction kites in light winds using an adapted version of the reverse landing on independent handles. Despite the different line attachment positions and the de-power system on the Sabre,

it's actually the same technique as for the other kites, just performed slightly differently.

- Either fly a low pass or bring the kite down the edge of the wind window towards your chosen landing spot.

- As the kite gets close to your landing spot, turn it as if to fly up the window again by pulling on one side of the bar.

- Quickly neutralise your steering and, holding the bar near its centre with one hand only, use the other hand to grab the rear lines leader line coming out of the centre eyelet of your bar and pull hard. This will fully engage the rear lines and bring the kite to rest on the ground on its trailing edge. Take a couple of steps towards the kite to make sure it stays landed. On the Sabre control bar the rear lines are attached to the bar tips, so to land your Sabre you need to grab the landing handle, situated on the safety leash at the point where it splits in two to attach to the rear lines. The safety leash should be hanging underneath the bar and flying lines. Pull the handle a metre towards you at the appropriate moment and it has the same effect, fully engaging the rear lines, killing the power and bringing the kite down on its trailing edge and back.

- Immobilise the kite by using a ground stake to peg the leash wrist strap down (keeping the rear lines engaged) then weighting the kite down with sand or whatever comes to hand.

In strong winds you won't be able to land by grabbing the rear leader line in that way as the kite will be pulling too hard. You'll be able to land using the kite's safety leash but you'll

still need to bring the kite out towards the edge of the window, until it comes to a position a couple of metres above the ground, leading edge facing the window edge.

- As the kite reaches the correct position prepare yourself to release the control bar. If you've been flying hooked into a harness you will need to unhook at this point.

- Release the bar from your hands and it will slide away from you along the centre leader line until it reaches its stop. The kite is retained by your wrist leash (you did remember to put your wrist leash on didn't you?), fully engaging the rear lines and fully releasing the front lines. The kite will instantly de-power and fall to the ground on its trailing edge.

- After the kite has landed you should walk a few steps backward to keep tension on the rear lines and prevent the kite blowing away. Immobilise it by pegging down the wrist leash strap with a ground stake and weighting down the kite with sand.

In very strong wind it may prove too difficult to solo land the kite using this method, in which case you will need a helper to grab the kite and immobilise it for you.

- Fly the kite carefully down one edge of the wind window as described.

- Steer the kite down near to the ground.

- Your helper should approach the kite from downwind, behind it, well clear of the flying lines. Keep the kite as still as possible close to the ground until they are able to grab one tip and then pull the kite down.

- As soon as your helper has grabbed the kite you should release the tension on the flying lines by taking a couple of steps forward towards the kite. Once the helper has immobilised the kite by weighting its upwind tip down with sand or whatever comes to hand you can stake down the control bar using the wrist leash strap.

RECOVERING THE KITE

Recovery and re-launch are straightforward. If your kite has landed right way up (leading edge pointing up) you can (re-)launch in the normal way, untwisting the flying lines first if necessary. If the kite comes down on its leading edge – upside down – you will need to roll the kite over so it's the right way up before you can launch.

- Reach forward with one hand and grab the rear lines leader line coming out of the front of the bar. On the Sabre, reach for the landing handle.

- Pull hard on the leader line or grab the handle and the kite will begin to reverse off the ground.

- At this point the Sabre will steadily flip over so it comes to rest on its trailing edge. Release the landing handle to bring tension back onto all four lines then (re-)launch in the normal way. Flying any of the other Flexifoil quad line kites, you must pull back on one side of the control bar as the kite reverses off the ground to make it turn

▶ De-power system: push the bar for less power, pull the bar for more power

and face upwards, coming to rest on its trailing edge. Release the rear lines leader line then (re-)launch in the normal way.

BEFORE WE MOVE ON...

In the following chapters we're going to look at applying your newly acquired kite skills to extreme power kite sports such as kiteboarding, landboarding, snowkiting etc. If you can launch, fly, position the kite where you want it, land and recover the kite, you've got a full hand of kite skills to get moving with. However, most of these activities will require you to wear a harness in order to deal with the extreme forces at play. Only when you've completely mastered quad line flying **without** a harness will it be time to get used to flying **with** one. You will need to fully familiarise yourself with harness flying before you try and hook onto some serious power and get moving, whether on land, water or snow. Here's a little quad line driving test to try with independent handles

(devised by American flyer David Brittain, one of the undisputed master quad line and power kite flyers of all time) to help you tell whether you're ready to try harness flying or not.

- Launch your kite, fly it to the zenith, stop and turn the kite to a vertical position (leading edge facing one side of the wind window), holding it still. This is the 12 o-clock position. Directly beneath it at ground level is the 6 o'clock position.

- One by one, fly your kite (holding it in its vertical axis) to each 'hour' point around the clock face, stopping it at the correct position, then flying back to the zenith, stopping and moving on to the next one… At 6 o'clock you should be able to hold the kite on one tip on the ground.

- Try this once with the kite facing left, then facing right.

- Once you can make the full 12 positions left and right without slip ups, you just might be ready for something a little more serious…

LET'S GET MOVING

5

> "Moving with the wind the first time you bomb down the beach is just awesome, and it helps amazingly for making the transition onto a kiteboard later.

ANDREYA WHARRY, FLEXIFOIL TEAM KITEBOARDER, EXTREME ACADEMY POWER KITE INSTRUCTOR

73

UNDERSTANDING 'APPARENT' WIND

Moving with wind power as a leisure pursuit (as opposed to actually needing to get from A to B), whichever way you do it, usually means trying to run backwards and forwards across the wind, not losing distance downwind, even going upwind and certainly being able to get back to your start point. After all, that's where your car is. Once you can do all that, in a sense you've 'graduated'. But there's an important factor that comes into play once you start moving forwards, across the wind, one you'll need to learn to deal with if you want to get that power kite mortar board. It's a phenomenon called 'apparent wind;' we've mentioned it in previous chapters and now it's time for a proper explanation.

Imagine you are standing on a board or sitting in a buggy, pointing at right angles to the wind (wind blowing from one side). The kite is above your head and if you steer it down the window edge, as you bring it in front of you, it powers up and it starts to pull you along. As you speed up though, the wind caused by your movement will appear to come more from in front of you, blowing into your face. The combination of the true wind and the wind from your forward motion is called the 'apparent' wind. Travelling at right angles to the true

wind, the apparent wind will increase the faster you go, causing the kite to pull harder, increasing your speed even more. Steering slightly upwind gives the optimum apparent wind, but be careful, steering too far upwind will cause you to lose power as a result. To complicate things still further, not only will apparent wind blow harder, it will come more from in front causing the kite to fly more downwind of you, to your side. The result of this could eventually be a big sideways skid or you being pulled over off your board or out of the buggy sideways. This is where real power kite skills come into play. You will have to learn to take pre-emptive action, 'working' the kite by moving it higher in the window to lose power and a little speed before powering up again to resume maximum speed. Or using your de-power system to ease off and re-position the kite. With practice you will sense in advance when is the right time to relax the pressure, before the apparent wind starts to have an adverse effect. A good plan would be to start your run aiming for a point just upwind of where you actually want to go to both to allow for this sideways pull and to get the maximum apparent wind effect. Kites which move around a lot (for example, two line kites) have a more variable apparent wind and less consistent power. That's why people switched in such overwhelming numbers to quad lines kites. Check the diagram on page 80, which shows the effect of apparent wind on a buggy but which applies to all kite traction disciplines.

◀ Kite buggying through the shore break
▶ Sand surfing on a kite landboard

TRACTION KITE SAFETY

Let's say this now because before you go anywhere near a kitebuggy or a board of any description, you need to understand a few things. Good traction kiting means safe and responsible traction kiting, because the

danger to yourself and other people is considerably increased. Do not attempt to board or buggy until you have fully mastered your kite. Never attach yourself permanently to the kite. Use extreme caution. Never use your board or buggy in conditions that are too extreme for your skill level and equipment. Never board or buggy if you cannot safely handle the power of your kite, use a smaller kite or wait for lighter wind. Avoid gusty winds, which can be very difficult for inexperienced flyers, even for experts. Avoid all other kite contra indications (lightning, power cables, roads, airports etc.). Always behave in a responsible manner and respect other site users. Always select a site with a big clear space all around you, free of people, obstructions and sharp objects. Always disable your kite and lines when not in use, avoid leaving unsecured kites on the ground and never leave them where other board or buggy riders are moving. Never board or buggy on busy beaches or bathing areas, or anywhere you could injure someone. Always obtain permission to use the site if appropriate. Respect nature, the site and other users at all times, and always clear up your rubbish. Check all your equipment regularly (kites, boards, buggy, flying lines, harness and other safety gear) before use. Do not use worn or damaged equipment: repair or replace it immediately. Always use appropriate safety equipment. Be aware of your flying lines at

◀Big air tricks like this one-foot toeside grab are for experts

all times; they can cause serious injury when under tension from a powered-up kite. Never allow inexperienced kite flyers to use your equipment. You are responsible at all times for the safe operation of your kite, board, buggy and other equipment. It is strongly recommended that you take out third party liability insurance that covers traction kiting. In short, use your common sense ! There will be plenty of adrenaline to come without taking unnecessary risks.

TRACTION ACTION

As previously mentioned, the first modern kite traction action to be invented was kite buggying, driving a three-wheeled buggy across hard sand or playing fields. Traction kiting has since diversified considerably, but the basic principle for all forms of kite traction is very similar, allowing for differences imposed by the type of vehicle, terrain and geographic and meteorological conditions. We'll look at buggying and other land kite sports in detail a little later, but once the basic principle of kite traction for wheeled transport became established, curiosity naturally drove people to experiment with various other dry land options. Kiteboarding was the first kiteboard sport to establish itself, but that took power kiting onto the water. Nowadays there's a dry landboard sport you can try, one that's really booming in popularity, as a sport in its own right but also as a

▶ Getting moving on a Flexifoil landboard

cheaper way of accessing the huge buzz of kiteboarding without going on the water…

1. KITE LANDBOARDING

"The most exciting thing about landboarding is that it's so new there's no one to copy, no pre-determined progression to follow; as soon as you're a competent rider you can start trying things no one else has even considered."

John Birnie, Flexifoil International sponsored kite landboarder

Like a big, off-road skateboard, landboards (also known as mountain or all-terrain boards) are great fun on any hard beach or big inland site with reasonably smooth terrain, playing fields being the obvious option. A beach, with its advantages of smooth open space and steady wind, is the ideal location to help you learn quickly. Confined spaces, bumpy surfaces and lumpy winds can make learning more difficult. As usual you need to be well away from other people and obstacles, with plenty of room downwind in case you are pulled forward. Protective equipment is recommended: elbow, wrist and knee guards, and a decent crash helmet. What you won't want to begin with is a harness, because if you are pulled over forwards, the hook and its fitting could cause you injury pushing back against and into your abdomen. Once you've

Landboarding (minus kite) has existed as a minority sport for a number of years (even more 'fringe' than power kiting) but the boards, already well technically advanced, have only relatively recently been harnessed to kite power. What was very much a minority activity in the traction kite scene as recently as 2001 is now one of the fastest growing. It's easy to understand. First, there's now a well-established board sport culture all over the world, and people are much more interested generally in all extreme boards / skis / skates / surf sports. Almost the same sentence can be used in relation to power kiting, bringing two powerful movements together in one sport. And there's that third factor: kiteboarding (on water) has become an international phenomenon, but getting the equipment together that you must have to kiteboard well and safely doesn't come cheap. Kite landboarding offers a lot of the same sensations – speed, power, jumps, adrenaline – on a vastly lower budget. Not least you'll need a lot less size of kite to get you moving fast on a landboard than on a kiteboard because the friction from those four small wheels is much less than that of the flat hull or hard edge of a kiteboard working into the water. And there's no need for expensive water re-launch capability for your kite, either. Not only that, the skills you learn in kite landboarding will be very useful if and when you do get out onto the water. The standard of the boards being manufactured today has developed almost as fast and as far as their water counterparts.

As with all kite traction sports, you'll be better off learning in a light to moderate wind where things will happen slower. You can afford to be much less powered up than for a buggy, one kite size at least, especially on hard flat sand, as the resistance from a mountain board is very low. Use a smaller kite to begin with as there will be less lateral pull and you should find it easier to stay up on the board. The **Rage**, **Blade** and **Sabre** are all suitable for kite landboarding.

Landboards are four-wheelers and are able to go in both directions, like a Twin Tip board for snowboarding. Just as Twin Tips have made learning to kiteboard a much easier prospect for legions of newcomers to that sport, so the four wheel landboard has become the essential tool for kite landboarders, eliminating the compulsory jibe (U-turn) that is a difficult stage in kite buggying and other board sports such as windsurfing, but also opening up a whole range of different trick possibilities. As with kiteboarding, the Twin Tip idea helps you get your fun fix faster.

THE FLEXIFOIL KITE LANDBOARD RANGE

Flexifoil was the first company in the world to release kite-specific landboards. The boards first appeared on the market in 2003 and were an instant hit. 2007's fourth generation

learned the basics you'll probably want to use a harness and it will certainly help get the centre of pull lower down hence reducing wasted effort = faster, more efficient boarding and less tired arms! For now, try with a small kite, that way you won't need the harness anyway.

▲ Top: Flexifoil Flexdeck
▲ Bottom: Flexifoil Airdeck

boards are the result of four years worth of rider feedback and R+D development.

Flexifoil currently manufactures two models of four wheeled kite landboards, each adapted to a specific performance requirement and skill level. The boards were designed by a specialist company, G2A, in association with Flexifoil. The G2A team are experts in working with carbon, composites and moulding. They're also serious power kiters and landboarders, so when they came up with their board designs it was a logical next step for them to take them to the experts in taking power kiting to the people, Flexifoil.

Apart from some radically cool deck and base (underside) decos, both boards have advantages and features specific to kiting which set them apart from existing landboards. Most striking is the innovative, asymmetric and ergonomic deck shape, which positions the rider off-centre to balance the sideways pull of the kite, taking the power of the kite and driving it through the board to deliver better upwind performance than a conventional (straight) board. Not only do the decks curve slightly up towards the front and back tips, viewed from above they have a cut away frontside edge with the backside edge curving equally outwards giving them a distinctive 'convex' arched shape as you will see from the photos. They are purpose built for kite landboarding and not suitable for conventional landboard downhilling. The boards have tough composite construction decks, 39cm axle width, strong five spoke nylon wheel hubs, cushioned, anti-slip deck pads and easy kick-off adjustable velcro footstraps

and come with a coil ankle leash as standard. The leash means that when you crash, your board won't inconvenience you by disappearing down the beach and won't present a possible risk to other landboarders.

The **Flexdeck** is a great all-purpose landboard that is excellent for beginners but which has the performance to interest more adventurous and experienced riders, a real all-rounder. It's great for jumping – and soft, cushioned landings – and gives an all-round smooth ride. It has a wood and glass-fibre deck, an intermediate wheel base length (92cm), skate trucks and new Flexifoil lightweight 20cm tyres and hubs, all of which make it an excellent board for carving, jumping and chilled out cruising. The Flexdeck gives you a well-balanced and controllable ride, even at speed. It's the best choice for powered-up beginners and intermediate riders. Fully fitted out it weighs in at 7kg.

The **Airdeck** is Flexifoil's radical trick machine and is for more advanced riding. At 82cm it's short and highly manoeuvrable, with touch-sensitive steering. It's the ideal board for any experienced rider looking for that bit of extra buzz to be had once you get into tricks and jumping. It's equipped with the same 20cm tyres and skate trucks but its smaller size and lower weight (6.5kg) means less drag in the air, maximising air time to make more radical tricks easier. The deck is wood/carbon composite and features special easy-grip, non-slip grip pads for board grabs, spins and flicks, plus grab-rails for grinding and 'board-offs'. The Airdeck gives you more possibility for technicality and

creativity, taking kite landboarding into the realms of pure freestyle.

There's a small amount of assembly to do when you get your Flexifoil landboard from the shop. Follow the manufacturer's instructions carefully and once you've got your board fully assembled, your kite set up and you're wearing the appropriate protective gear, you're ready to start experiencing the big buzz of kite landboarding.

Getting started...

Your final check before getting on the board is to see if you are 'regular' or 'goofy'. If you've already done board sports you know about it. It describes which foot you prefer to place forwards when you stand to ride a board. Everyone's got a 'stronger' side; if you don't know yours, have a friend shove you in the back when you're not expecting it. Whichever foot you use to save yourself is your lead foot and the other is the supporting foot. Goofy is right foot forward, regular left foot forward. Start off by going towards your good side to make it easier but don't forget that to come back the other way you'll be riding to your 'weaker' side, which might be difficult at first but should come quickly with practice. It'll have to! Set up your board pointing towards your good side, downwind across the window, at 45 degrees to the wind direction. This will allow you to get the board moving easily before you turn to steer more across the wind:

■ Launch your kite and fly it up to the minimum power position at the zenith.

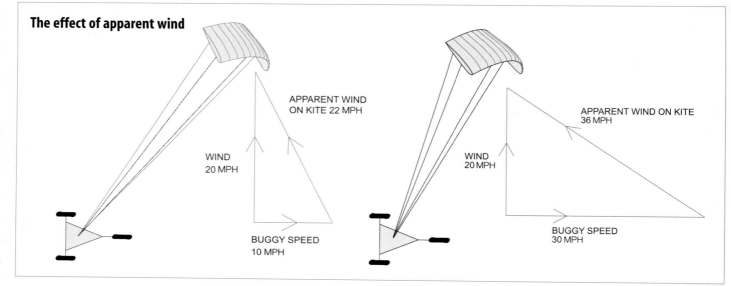

The effect of apparent wind

APPARENT WIND
ON KITE 22 MPH

WIND
20 MPH

BUGGY SPEED
10 MPH

APPARENT WIND ON KITE
36 MPH

WIND
20 MPH

BUGGY SPEED
30 MPH

■ You will need to approach the board from one side or the other. From upwind means you can see where you're putting your feet better, important if you've got bindings to get into, but could trip over the board if pulled by a gust. From down-wind means no tripping over but not seeing where you put your feet so well. Try both to see which you find easiest. Put your front foot in its strap first then the rear, keeping the kite high.

■ Once on the board bring the kite slightly back, across the top of the wind window away from the direction you wish to go. Then turn the kite back the other way, div-ing it down slightly into the wind window to power up, then towards the side of the wind you wish to move towards, taking care not to bring the kite too low and risk being pulled off by excess lateral pull as a result. The board should start moving

towards the kite and keep moving towards it as long as you keep the kite there. There's a lot of body work to be done to get your correct balance for riding and levering against the kite so you'll need a good flexed position, knees and arms slightly bent.

■ Start by steering slightly downwind to get some momentum (not too far downwind or you'll de-power the kite) before gradually easing yourself onto a cross-wind reach. Do this by transferring weight slightly onto your heels, leaning slightly back. Once you hit the direction you want, ease off the heel pres-sure a little to hold the board on a straight line with pressure from your leading foot.

■ You can slow down any time by taking the kite higher in the wind window (and using heel pressure to steer upwind) but you'll need to shift your balance to allow for the reduced pull.

■ You will frequently find you need to 'work' the kite in an 'S' pattern up and down the window. This applies to marginal wind situations (wind at the lower limit of the kite's wind range) or simply just to get /orkeep going. It's done by applying alter-nate left and right pulls to the control bar or handles, not too hard, just enough to keep the kite moving up and down the edge of the window, powering up as it dives, losing power as it climbs.

In an ideal world, one with smooth, steady (strong enough) wind and a good under-standing of what you're doing, you can 'lock' the kite in position near the edge of the wind window and enjoy the ride. But remember the apparent wind factor we explained ear-lier. The stronger the wind and faster you decide to go, the greater the apparent wind.

You will need to adjust the board's steering and move the kite up the window slightly to compensate. That's really what's meant by 'working the kite', bringing it lower to power up, higher to ease off. Your first runs will inevitably take you downwind, leaving you with a walk back to regain lost ground, but all being well it shouldn't take much time before you learn to hold a cross wind reach fairly comfortably. Either way, that will bring another couple of issues up, those of stopping and turning round to come back.

You'll quickly notice, and you'll already know if you've come from a skateboard or mountainboard background, that when you shift your weight to lean either forwards or backwards on the board, the effect is to turn it. If you're riding regular, leaning forwards will turn you to your right and leaning back will turn you left (vice versa for goofy riders). It's the land equivalent of front and backside carving on a kiteboard or snowboard. Leaning backwards against the pull of the kite feels more 'natural' whereas shifting your weight forwards with the pull to ride more frontside feels less secure. Experiment while not too powered-up at first, with small 'weaves' during your runs, gently slaloming the board between an imaginary set of cones by using alternate heel and toe side pressure. Keep the kite relatively high on your frontside carves to avoid having to lean too far forward. As your skill level and confidence grows you'll be able

▶ Flexifoil's Sabre is specifically designed for land-boarding and snowkiting

to gradually carve faster, harder and more aggressively, using more sustained kite power through the turns, compensating with your body strength and more accentuated lean.

Turning round...

A kite landboard board is a Twin Tip, it's got symmetrical ends, so you can take advantage of its reversibility when it comes to turning round. Getting going Twin Tip style means you get express delivery of your fun while you take your time learning more complicated frontside carving and riding later on. All you really need do to reverse your direction on a twin tip, four wheel board is to slow down, stop, then power up again in the opposite direction.

■ As you ride along bring the kite up the edge of the wind window where it will act as a brake, slowing you down. Shift your weight slightly to the centre of the board and lean back a little to turn upwind.

■ Fly the kite across the top of the wind window, turning it to point the other way. Be careful not to move the kite behind you yet, that might lead to an unexpected jump or worse.

■ As the board slows down to a stop, bring your weight over onto your 'good' foot so you are now leading with your 'bad' one.

■ Dive the kite down into the power zone as you did before, this time facing the other way, and it will power up again and start pulling you forwards on your return run. Your board is already pointing slightly downwind (the effect of turning upwind

going the other way) to help get you moving again.

■ Now you can keep working the kite or 'lock' it at the appropriate place for your return reach if the wind is strong enough, likewise using heel pressure to work the board and adjust your steering. It's all in the timing again and practice will make for neater and more aggressive changes of direction without waiting for the board to stop, even adding a small jump (see later) to help you through the transition...

Your other option for turning 180 degrees is actually an advanced manoeuvre for later on (there are other, more important things to learn first) as it involves coming out of the turn riding frontside (toeside). Sounds confusing? Let's talk you through it now although you may not put it into practice for a while. You're on a good straight run across the wind…

- Transfer weight towards your toes and the board will begin to turn downwind, towards the kite. Go carefully, not too much weight too quickly. You are aiming to do a wide, carving, downwind turn that will avoid going so far or fast downwind that you de-power the kite.

- As you begin to turn the board, fly the kite up the edge of the window, turning it to point the other way and bringing it across the high part of the window to begin pulling you in the opposite direction, quickly enough to keep tension on the flying lines but not so fast that the kite pulls you off sideways before you've got through the turn. Try to drive through the turn quickly enough to avoid advancing too far towards the kite downwind, otherwise you risk de-powering the kite which may then fall down uncontrollably in the wind window before suddenly powering up close to the ground, right in the middle of the power zone. Expect a big wipe-out if that happens.

- Keep the weight on your toes as the board comes round 180 degrees, but use some heel pressure to start straightening out from the carve.

- As the kite comes over to the side of the wind window you wish to travel towards, dive it down to power up again. As it does so you will accelerate forwards, back the way you came.

- Keep your weight over your toes, leaning slightly forward, flying the kite over your leading shoulder (which one that is depends on which way you were travelling when you initiated the turn).

- Once you're powered-up again properly you can continue your toe-side run or 'transition' the board back round again by quickly raising it off the ground and half-rotating your hips back round to a 'normal' position while keeping the kite high in the window. Land your rear wheels first for the smoothest landing and get your kite powered up again quickly. As soon as you land lean away from the kite slightly to help keep tension on the flying lines.

It's all a question of timing and the more you practise the better your timing will be and you'll be able to make the whole thing in one sweeping movement. Don't go for it too powered up at first but aim to keep the board moving all through the turn. If you do stop it will be difficult to keep your balance and power up again riding frontside. The advantage of this type of turn is that you keep moving all through the turn. The disadvantage is that you're now flying over your lead shoulder with your back to the kite and your weight forwards. It needs good balance and feel for the kite and will require some practice to get right.

As you build your skill range you'll become aware that it's possible to carve a frontside turn, starting off riding frontside and shifting your balance completely from front to backside as you drive through it. Toeside riding is an advanced move though, not one you'll try as a beginner when you'll have plenty to deal with mastering the basics. Whichever way you're doing it, with practice you'll be able to make your turns faster and more aggressive, losing less power and speed. Before we take a look at another advanced move – making your first jumps – let's cover the other essential basic manoeuvre.

Stopping…

The simplest way to stop your landboard is, as explained, to steer the kite up to the zenith and keep it there while you slow to a stop. Steering the board slightly upwind helps but won't stop you suddenly, on the spot. It's ok for when you're just starting out and only moving slowly, but as you begin to build up speed on your runs you'll want and indeed need a faster, more efficient braking and stopping move.

- You are reaching across the wind at reasonable speed. Bring your body to a more upright position and steer the kite to the edge of the window, high up towards the top. This helps slow it down and de-powers slightly.

- As you do so, start applying pressure on the board with your heels to turn the board upwind, keeping the kite high, near the middle of the wind window pointing straight upwards (but don't let it get behind you) where it will brake your forward speed.

You may feel the wheels skid sideways at first (a power skid!) but with good, even foot pressure you will slow down.

- Lean slightly against the pull of the kite and move it right to the top of the window or zenith, steering your board as far upwind as possible to bring you to a full stop.

With practice you'll be able to make the stop much more aggressive, moving the kite slightly earlier and more quickly, driving the board harder with your legs. Be careful never to let the kite get behind you or too low down, leading to either an involuntary jump or you being pulled backwards off the board.

Getting upwind...

One of the drags about learning traction kiting is that you do a lot of travelling downwind with an inevitable walk-back at the end of it. With practice you'll be able to go backwards and forwards across the wind so you don't lose ground. In time you'll want to be able to get upwind, not just to recover ground lost jumping etc., but to get away from all the beginners clogging up the centre and downwind sections of your flying spot.

It goes without saying that you'll need to consciously steer upwind to be able to get there, but there are important considerations to bear in mind. To be able to steer more aggressively, i.e. upwind, you'll need to be less aggressive with your kite. Too low down or powered up and it will be hard for you to hold

▶ Kite landboarding is more suited to control bar flying

that upwind course, there's so little resistance from the wheels (this is less of a problem on water where there's much greater resistance). And you must avoid steering too far upwind or you will simply slow down to a stop and lose all your ground getting going slightly downwind again. Apparent wind will reduce because you're moving slower so there's less risk of side sliding downwind but also less power and momentum to help boost you along. Getting upwind requires a good kite, a good board, and a good understanding of how to 'work' your kite to maximise forward movement while reducing lateral, downwind pull, not an easy balance to strike and one you'll have to work at to master. It's an impor-

tant lesson to learn though if, for instance, you want to get into really serious stuff like jumping !

Jumping...

The real adrenaline factor kites add to landboarding, as they do to kiteboarding, is the ability to get seriously airborne. Jumping could be done for any number of reasons: a simple transition; a low spin (front or back) ; getting onto a slider or grind rail; big air or hang time; aerial gymnastics and serious tricks like grabs, board flips, board-offs ; jumping out of trouble... Here we'll take you through how to execute a simple, basic jump, from a cross wind reach, up and down again, back onto the same cross

wind reach. Anything more serious should be left until afterwards when you've fully mastered basic jumping and – perhaps more importantly – landing your board again safely…

If you were paying attention earlier you'll remember we spoke about involuntary jumps happening when you take the kite too far behind you when braking or stopping. Controlled, intentional jumping is different, not least because you'll want to keep moving through and after the jump. There are three main elements to jumping: approach or take-off, air-time and landing. You will need good, confident kite control and it may be worthwhile practicing the kite movements off the board first to be sure of what you're doing. If you're using a kite with a de-power system you can hook into the harness loop and stay hooked in through the jump. It'll be essential for more advanced hands-free, no-hands or board-off jumps you may want to progress to later. De-power or not, if you don't have a quick release safety system do not hook in, you need to be able to detach yourself from the kite in case of a problem.

- Get back on that cross-wind reach and build up speed and power, both in the kite and in your board (try driving slightly more upwind), working against the pull with your body and ready to spring into your jump.

- Start moving your kite slightly back into the power zone then up the window to the zenith (leading edge pointing up, but never behind you), faster than you would do for a stop manoeuvre, to generate good lift.

◀ You need big power and a stable kite for big jumps

- You will feel the kite lift you and your board; this is the moment to spring into the jump to help get you off the ground. A small amount of pressure with your 'front' hand will help stabilise the kite at the zenith, but not too much or you risk powering up again too soon. Concentrate on jumping up, the wind and your forward speed will give your jump some carry. Try to keep your board straight and not let it 'flap' with wind drag.

- Once you sense the jump peaking, start looking forwards (the direction you were travelling before you launched the jump) and down at the ground to 'spot' your rough landing position. Some more front hand pressure on the control bar at this point will start moving the kite forwards and down in the window to help you land with some power in the kite, not too low though or you will slam down hard.

- As you reach landing try and point the board slightly downwind to help you get moving again smoothly, bend your knees to absorb the impact and try to land the back wheels slightly before the front ones, as an aeroplane would.

- If you've made it this far, now's the time to lean back and steer slightly upwind again to help power up the kite and get back onto a reach. And if you enjoyed that, why not try another ?

It may take a while to get the complete jump cleanly executed; don't worry that's perfectly normal. Make sure you're properly protected because the chances are you're going to have some crashes as you learn. Don't go too big too soon, learn the technique under medium power before you try with a big powered-up kite. You quickly realise that even small jumps feel huge to begin with, it's already a big enough buzz and once you've mastered this initial stage there's plenty more adrenaline to be unleashed. Remember the mantra: safety is the responsibility of the flyer. Above all, remember that your jumps will always take you downwind. Make sure there's plenty of space downwind and in front of your direction of travel before you attempt any jump. You're the one taking the risk and you must never put others at risk through ill-considered riding.

Practise your range of basic landboard skills until you're really confident; they're the basic tools you need to unlock the sport. You'll be able to move in both directions side to side plus up and downwind, stop, turn and turn round, hit a basic jump and land it again. Think about taking a course at one of the many power kite schools there are now: hands-on, informed, structured training will help speed up your learning processes. You'll need at least two sizes of kite if you want to landboard often, a medium sized kite for light winds plus a smaller one for medium to strong winds. And you'll be amazed at how soon you can start hitting decent speed and the aggressive carving you'll be able to achieve, and what an amazing buzz it is when you're leaning hard and hand dragging like a pro. Now get out there!

▶ Flexifoil landboards are built for radical action

2. KITE BUGGYING

"I was ecstatic when I realised I'd got my kite buggy idea to work. I was belting along this beach wondering if I was finally going to be able to quit my boring office job. I never dreamed the same basic design would still be going strong more than twenty years later. Buggying's a fantastic buzz, and it helps amazingly for making the transition onto a kiteboard."

Peter Lynn, power kite and kite buggy pioneer designer

The idea is very simple. Fly a large single kite or stack of smaller ones, sufficient to generate enough power to pull yourself along. Sit in your vehicle and manipulate them in such a way as to drive yourself around. A modern power kite and kite buggy are sophisticated adrenaline sport tools, specifically designed for the job, generating speeds up to 60 mph, the result of more than 15 years of intensive commercial research and development. When you sit down in a kite buggy with the control handles or bar in your hands you know you're in for a thrill and it's an immense buzz, travelling low down, open to the elements. Even your first 5mph run feels like 50. A bang-up-to date toy in all respects, but moving around by kite power is by no means an original idea. The use of kite power on a wheeled vehicle is anything but new. During the late 18th century, in the south west of England around Bristol, inventor George Pocock was experimenting with kite traction using large single line kites attached to a passenger carriage, big enough to carry horses in a special compartment to use if the wind dropped.

Two hundred years later, long-standing kite traction addict and pioneer, New Zealander Peter Lynn, was widely credited with being the inventor of a successful modern kite vehicle. This time the concept was a single seat 'buggy' or 'kart', three-wheeled with the lone driver sitting low to the ground over the rear axle, flying the kite with his hands and steering the single front wheel with his feet. And this time the kite was a modern, two-lined, soft aerofoil kite, in Lynn's case called a Peel, on account of its pointed, eliptical shape, making it resemble a slice of orange peel. The buggy frame was made from stainless steel and used high quality bearings. Its simple 'basket' style webbing seat made it very easy to be pulled out of the buggy leading to many spectacular wipe outs. The kites weren't specifically designed for the job, they just happened to be what was available at the time. Kite power existed and people were hunting around for something to do with it. The whole package was far from perfect but, nevertheless, kite buggying was born and has not in essence changed format since, despite the many makes of buggies and traction kites there are on the market today.

The first Lynn buggies appeared in the mid to late 1980s and for various cost and practical reasons the buggy scene grew painfully slowly for a while, but grow it steadily did. Then, in 1992 the first soft quad line ram air kites appeared and other kite and buggy manufacturers were starting to get involved as the sales volumes slowly increased and shop prices therefore dropped. Large production-run buggy designs at cheaper prices were hitting the shops by 1994, then Ray Merry and Cobra Kites launched their Skytiger four line buggy kite in 1995 and suddenly buggying took off big time.

The surge of interest in the mid 1990s brought in new and different ideas and equipment developed fast. Despite the rapid opening up of the power kite market, manufacturers such as Peter Lynn and Flexifoil have been at the forefront of the whole traction scene, supporting events and organisations, sponsoring drivers (and now kiteboarders) etc. Products have developed at an astonishing rate and kite buggying is vastly more sophisticated nowadays. Saying that, it's worth noting that despite various attempts to develop and improve it, Lynn's original three-wheeled buggy idea is still the most common basic buggy design almost 20 years since its conception.

The first Flexifoil branded buggies appeared shortly after Lynn's original commercial models (coincidentally designed by Lynn himself) and since that time they've been joined by many other manufacturers. That competition has been good for the overall buggy market, pushing standards and performance to ever-higher degrees. Modern production buggies are designed for even more extreme usage, specially speed racing and jumping or freestyling with the buggy. Race buggies tend to have wider rear axles and often the wheels angled slightly to improve stability at high speed; Freestylers are shorter, tighter turning and stronger to cope with heavy landings. You'll find there's a host of accessories available for you to customise your buggy for different terrains, meaning that a standard production buggy can be tuned for beginners and pros alike.

Flexifoil's latest buggy is a great all-rounder, designed by Rob Hills – one of the world's top extreme, freestyle buggy drivers – and crammed full of performance features and extras: an adjustable downtube on the front fork to cater for different sizes of rider; curved foot rests to help keep your feet in position; hi-grade wide stainless steel tube frame for strength and stability ; a wrap around seat and contoured frame for comfort and back support; stainless steel bolts and specially engineered fittings; a splashguard for muddy fields and dirty beaches; and, new for 2006, a belly pan to protect the driver. The ideal buggy to max your fun whatever your level.

Buggying's natural beach habitat, plus the fact that Britain is a relatively small country geographically speaking, with lots of coastline, means wherever you are in the country,

▶ Ideal protective wear for traction kiting

in theory you're no more than five hours' drive from the sea, big empty beaches and a potential kitebuggy playground. Not much can match the pleasure of hurtling through the foaming shore break on a seriously powered-up buggy!

GETTING STARTED

You'll want the right kind of kite for buggying and what that almost certainly means is: four lines so you can 'lock' the kite in the power zone and regulate the power by changing the angle of attack, relatively thin profile to reduce lateral pull, a big wind window to make getting back upwind easier, mobile around the window to guarantee continuous access to maximum power, good edge handling and performance,

and smooth (as opposed to abrupt) acceleration to reduce the tendency to pull the driver out of the buggy. It's going to make the whole process a lot easier if you have a kite appropriate to your ability; there's no point buying a Ferrari if you've no idea how to drive yet. Be honest about your skill level; if you're a beginner, try an appropriate level kite first, for instance a small to medium sized **Rage**. Once you've learned enough you might want to progress onto a higher performance **Blade**, if anyone can get you off your Rage that is.

It's possible to learn buggying on your own, after all, the people who invented it had to make it up as they went along, but a good idea might be to try one of the increasing numbers of Flexifoil-approved buggy or wind sport schools (you'll find

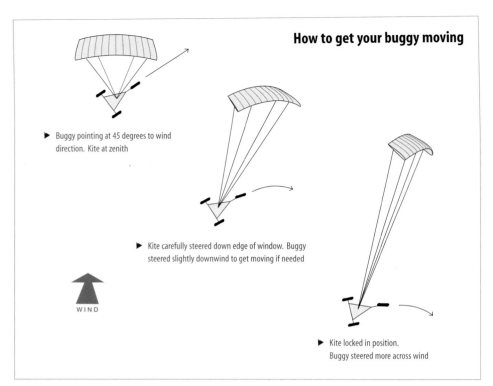

How to get your buggy moving

▶ Buggy pointing at 45 degrees to wind direction. Kite at zenith

▶ Kite carefully steered down edge of window. Buggy steered slightly downwind to get moving if needed

WIND

▶ Kite locked in position. Buggy steered more across wind

them on the Flexifoil website) where you can learn the basics and try out the equipment in complete (and insured!) safety, before committing your cash. If you're going to become a buggyer though you're going to need a buggy of your own at some point and hopefully it will be a Flexifoil model.

Follow the instructions correctly for assembling your buggy. Make sure the wheels are tightly bolted on and the tyres inflated to the correct pressure. There are two different

▲ Jumping with a harness leaves hands free for grabs

widths of tyre you can fit. The most versatile are the standard wide ones. Wide wheels spread the load over a wide area and prevent the buggy sinking in the sand. Even so, for very soft sand you might one day want to invest in a set of giant extra-wide 'big foot' wheels which can be fitted onto your buggy, though this might require a change of rear axle and front fork. You might want to change to an extra wide axle anyway, which improves stability, upwind performance and is great for racing.

Like all aspects of power kiting you are

better advised to start learning in a light to moderate wind, no more than 15mph, as the kite will pull less and everything will happen more slowly. You'll be multi-functioning and there's a serious brain overload to begin with as you get used to controlling the kite and buggy simultaneously, so slowing everything down a bit can really help. Check the wind direction carefully, specially if you're using a coastal site. The best wind on a beach will be an onshore, coming onto the beach from the sea. Not only will it be smooth, but since the aim will be to 'sail' backwards and forwards across the wind it will allow you to run up and down the length of the beach and keep you out of the water. An offshore wind will probably be lumpy and drive you out into the water more. A cross or side wind is the least preferred option, unless you're on a beach with significant depth at low tide. Find a good open space well away from other site users. Especially while you're learning and can't fully control what you do, you don't want to annoy people whose advice you'll be asking later. Here's how it should happen :

■ Your buggy should be pointing at 45 degrees to the wind direction, downwind to help you get going. Once the buggy is moving you will be trying to steer across the wind so as not to lose too much ground forwards. You can run downwind but you're going to have a long and uncomfortable walk back carrying all that equipment with the wind against you.

Your first objective is to learn how to buggy across the wind.

- Launch your kite and take it to the minimum power position at the zenith while you approach the buggy from the downwind side. This is to avoid you suddenly being pulled forward by a big gust causing you to fall on the buggy.

- Keeping the kite at the zenith, straddle the buggy and sit down in it. At this point you still have some resistance from your feet.

- Put one foot (upwind) on its foot peg, the other still holding you from being pulled forward.

- You are committed to going towards the side the buggy is pointing so dive the kite down slightly into the window to generate some power, and towards the corresponding edge of the window. Never take the kite back to the other (rear) side of the window as this will result in you being pulled backwards out of the buggy.

- As you feel the power coming into the kite lift your other foot up onto its foot peg and continue to steer slightly downwind to get the buggy moving.

- If there's good steady wind you will be able to 'lock' the kite in position at roughly 45 degrees to the ground and keep tension on the flying lines as the buggy gets going to avoid running over your own lines. Otherwise you'll need to 'work' the kite in that 'S' pattern, up and down near the window edge to try to adjust your steering to head more cross wind to help generate more apparent wind from your movement.

- Now try to steer the buggy more aggressively, slightly upwind (but not too far up or it will slow you down), which will help power up the kite more (the apparent wind factor). Remember to watch where you're going as well as the kite. You need 100% confidence in your kite skills so you can deal with where the buggy is going. You should be flying on the front lines mostly, just using the rear lines to keep the tension and hold the kite in position. If you're going too fast or feel there's too much power, take the kite further up the wind window, which will reduce power and slow you down.

The tuning of your quad line kite becomes quickly apparent, giving, if correctly set up, the ability to hit the brakes very hard for an instant de-power, even to land the kite if it all gets too much. But more significantly, it's the quad line control that allows you to lock the kite in position where a dual line kite, for instance, would be moving around all the time and make the buggy driving learning process more difficult. That's why quad line kites are so effective and so popular, helping you reduce the brain overload and concentrate more on buggying. If your kite has trouble either moving forward or backward, check the kite tuning section of your instruction manual.

STOPPING THE BUGGY

- While driving along across, down or upwind, start steering the kite up the edge of the wind window towards the zenith, pointing straight up. At the same time start steering the buggy a little upwind. The kite will begin to lose power and the buggy slow down. Don't let the kite get behind you or you risk being pulled backwards out of the buggy.

- Stop the kite high up in the centre window pointing upwards (not across the window) and steer the buggy a little more upwind. The more you resist the kite the more you slow down. You will come to a stop with the kite flying over your shoulder and above your head, in the minimum power position.

It's not a car, remember, you don't just hit the brakes and wait for the ABS to kick in. It will be more of a gradual slowing down at first. It's all a question of timing and one part in particular of the timing is crucial. With the kite flying behind you there is a big possibility you will be pulled out of the buggy, or along in the buggy, backwards. Take the kite too quickly behind you, too far behind or with too much power and you will suddenly find yourself reversing or being pulled out backwards.. The only thing then is to try and land the kite (easier said than done, travelling backwards at 15mph with your head banging on the ground) or let go of it altogether and use your safety leash to de-power it.

A quicker stop can be made with practice. It involves the same basic manoeuvre but done at more speed and with more aggressive steering of the buggy and kite. The main thing is to try steering the kite

slightly more behind you at the top of the wind window and to do it fractionally (but fractionally) earlier, at the same time turning the buggy more aggressively upwind into a skid and quickly applying opposite lock. At speed you slide the buggy to a stop facing upwind. Trying the power stop means stopping with more power in the kite for you to lean against and hence there is more possibility of being pulled backwards out of the buggy. It's a more advanced technique so build the power and speed up sensibly and progressively and avoid trying to learn in strong wind. And you'll need to keep a careful eye on your kite all the time once you've stopped or it may power up again unexpectedly.

Your ultimate sanction for stopping is to drop your control handles, releasing the kite and its pressure and allowing the buggy to roll gently to a stop. This should only be used as a last resort. Your kite comes with a safety leash. This means that as long as you are using the safety leash you can let go completely of your handles, safe in the knowledge that the kite will first de-power and second, return to ground with minimal risk to yourself and others. Recovering and re-launching the kite afterwards is relatively simple although there is a risk you might run over your own lines and tangle them on your axle. Always attach your safety leash(es) before bug-

◀ Independent handles compensate for the buggy driver's more restricted body movement

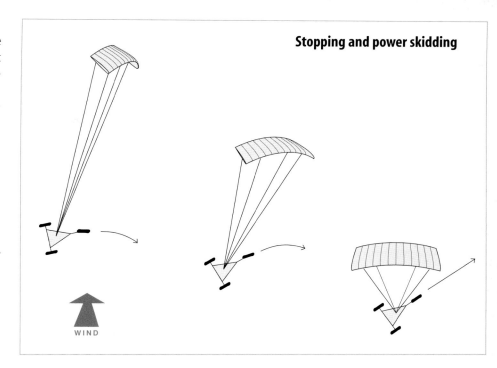

Stopping and power skidding

WIND

gying and practise your emergency drill before you have to use it for real. Even the pro pilots can get into difficulty and they would be the first to stress the importance of safe buggying. You can rip open the Velcro strap to detach the safety leash as a final option but this means releasing your kite completely. Apart from all the obvious safety issues, your quad line set spaghetti-d round someone else's axles or flying lines is normally considered a gross breach of buggy etiquette.

You may occasionally be forced to stop anyway if your kite becomes waterlogged, either from rain, spray or some unintention-

al landings on the wet part of the beach. It will no longer fly correctly, if at all. No option here, you must take it back somewhere dry, dry it out thoroughly and empty any sand out from inside before re-launching.

POWER SLIDES OR SKIDS

Once you've mastered the power stop, why not try a few power skids, the buggy equivalent of the hand-brake turn. You're probably going to end up doing a few inadvertently anyway, taking into account the effect of apparent wind as described earlier, that moment when the kite is flying so far down-

How to turn your buggy around

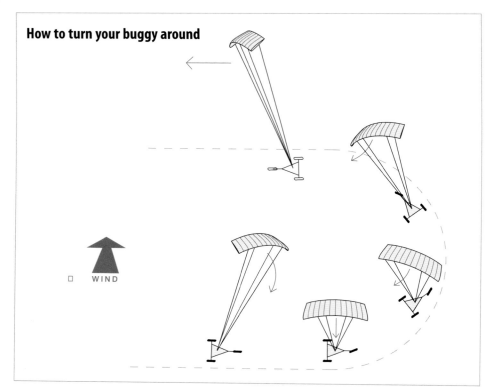

WIND

JIBING: TURNING THE BUGGY ROUND

We're talking about the necessary ability to turn the buggy through 180 degrees to go back the way you came which, no matter how good a time you're having buggying off into the sunset, you will have to do sometime. We mentioned going backwards and forwards, this is the 'back' bit. And thinking about it, it's not at all obvious. The kite's in front of you, nicely powered-up, you're rattling along but you can't just 'twin tip' as you can on a landboard. What do you do to get your buggy turned round and kite back to the other side of the wind window without being pulled out of the buggy? And which way do you turn the buggy anyway, up or downwind? My car's four miles back up the beach. Help!

Technically you can turn up or downwind but upwind is an advanced technique so we'll concentrate on the easier downwind version. Like all manoeuvres, it's one that needs good timing and adjustment all the way through. The first and most important thing you'll need to adjust is your forward speed. You can't really learn how to turn going in at full speed so you'll need to lose some before you go in. The main thing to remember is always to turn downwind, towards the kite, so you steer slightly upwind before you turn. Second, you need to turn the buggy as quickly as possible to avoid travelling towards and de-powering your kite. Actually turning the buggy is very easy as your feet are steering directly through the front wheel. There's no counter steering against the pull.

wind of you that you are pulled sideways in a big skid, fighting with opposite lock on your steering. And if you've already tried power stopping you'll already have a good grasp of the mechanics.

- Drive the buggy on a reach across the wind with the kite powered-up at 45 degrees to the ground near the edge of the wind window.

- Begin flying the kite up the window and slightly behind you as for a power stop. At the same time slam the buggy into an aggressive upwind turn and immediately reverse lock your steering.

- Keep the kite slightly less behind than you would to come to a stop and then turn it back towards the edge of the window it was on (towards the direction of travel), diving it down into the window to power up again and keep tension on the flying lines.

- As the kite powers up again ease off your full steering lock and let the buggy get going again slightly downwind to allow it to pick up speed before turning back onto a cross-wind reach.

- You are driving your buggy on a cross wind reach with the kite powered-up and at roughly 45 degrees to the ground. Start steering the buggy slightly up-wind and the kite up the edge of the wind window towards the zenith. The power eases off a little and the buggy starts to lose speed.

- You're ready to make your turn. Steer the kite quickly back up the wind window and across the top of it. At the same time steer the buggy hard into the turn. You need to use full lock to drive the buggy through the turn quickly.

- As the buggy comes round 180 degrees and is pointing back the way you came, dive the kite down slightly to the other side of the wind window (your new direction of travel) to power it up again and drive you through and out of the turn.

- Let the buggy get going again downwind slightly, then start steering it more across and upwind, and steer the kite to the correct position to 'work' it or 'lock' it for your return reach. Be ready for the pull coming back on as the kite powers back up again.

There's a fine balance to strike to make a good turn. You must slow down beforehand but above all you want to go in with enough speed to get all the way through the turn in one hit. If the buggy stops moving when you're face on to the kite, for instance, then the moment when the kite powers up again you could be yanked face forwards out of and

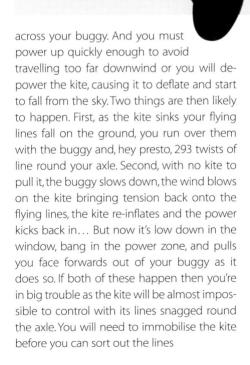

▶ Flexifoil kite buggies are super tough

across your buggy. And you must power up quickly enough to avoid travelling too far downwind or you will de-power the kite, causing it to deflate and start to fall from the sky. Two things are then likely to happen. First, as the kite sinks your flying lines fall on the ground, you run over them with the buggy and, hey presto, 293 twists of line round your axle. Second, with no kite to pull it, the buggy slows down, the wind blows on the kite bringing tension back onto the flying lines, the kite re-inflates and the power kicks back in... But now it's low down in the window, bang in the power zone, and pulls you face forwards out of your buggy as it does so. If both of these happen then you're in big trouble as the kite will be almost impossible to control with its lines snagged round the axle. You will need to immobilise the kite before you can sort out the lines

Most people's problems with turning arise from lack of forward speed going in (causing them to stop) or from going too far downwind in the turn. With practice you'll be able to make your turns faster, keeping the kite moving all through the move and with more power, and clearly you're going to need to practise turning to both sides.

Power kite guru David Brittain has developed a brilliant five step learning system for would-be buggy drivers which, with his kind permission, we're including here. It worked for me so I can recommend it, and it's incredibly simple. You only progress a step when you've fully mastered the one before.

Step 1: learn to fly your quad line kite with accurate enough control to be able to position it at the zenith (12 o-clock) and fly it to each 'hour' point in turn to both sides, return-

ing each time to 12 (see 'Quad-Line Kites' chapter).

Step 2: set out two cones on the ground about 50 metres apart, across the wind; 'walk' a figure eight between and around the two cones imagining and visualising manoeuvring the kite as you would in a buggy and making downwind turns round each cone.

Step 3: same thing but now you really do fly the kite, wearing and hooking into your harness if you wish, using the kite's power to pull you round the course.

Step 4: learn to make the same figure eight round the cones, now sitting in the buggy, but without the kite, so you'll need someone to push you, but practising the control

▲ Kite buggying with a control bar

movements with your hands to get the kite and buggy theory synch-ed.

Step 5: put the whole thing together, driving the buggy using the kite to pull you, using the smallest kite you have that will actually move you in the buggy; this will teach you how to 'work' a kite for power.

A couple of steady afternoons spent learning all that and then making some longer runs will build your confidence and teach you how to control and use your kite's power. And you'll need all of that when it comes to learning your final essential manoeuvre…

GETTING UPWIND

Once you've established enough control over what you're doing in the buggy to be

able to reach backwards and forwards across the wind you will want to learn how to turn that into steady upwind tacking, either for racing or simply to avoid the dreaded 'long walk back'. However well you learn to get upwind it is likely to be slow progress getting there and you must be patient and prepared to work the kite and buggy to get where you want to go. Be aware also that some kite designs are better able to get you upwind than others. Flexifoil's high performance traction kites are designed to help you get back upwind smoothly and easily.

Getting back upwind is the hardest thing to learn as a buggy driver so if you find it difficult at first, stick with it because patience will definitely bring its rewards. Initially, as you learn to drive you will find that your reaches take you gradually downwind. To get back upwind you will need to steer more aggressively with your feet, trying to keep the buggy pointing slightly upwind on each tack. To avoid slowing down too much or even stopping you must be less aggressive with the kite. You need to keep the kite less powered up by keeping or working it higher than normal on the edge of the wind window. If the kite is too low in the sky or too powered-up you will find it hard to gain ground because of the apparent wind factor.

There's a fine balance to achieve because if you're travelling too slowly and haven't got enough power you'll also find it difficult. This is particularly so during the turn at the end of each tack. The turns are made downwind as normal and if you lose speed or stop during your turn you're going to have to give up some of your hard won ground upwind going slightly downwind to get the buggy moving again. You need to make the turns as tight as possible, if you can, steering a little more upwind just before the turn and turning through more than 180 degrees to get on another upwind tack. If it sounds difficult that's because it is. But once you've mastered this you've got a full hand of essential buggy manoeuvres; not least you'll be able to get upwind, away from all those beginners clogging up the downwind space...

ESSENTIAL LANDBOARDING AND BUGGYING EQUIPMENT

There's an awful lot more to good landboarding and buggying than simply having a kite and a buggy. There are all sorts of other bits and pieces you might want to have that will make your sport easier and more enjoyable. But it's not simply a question of fun. First and foremost there's the safety aspect, protecting yourself and others from the worst-case scenario because you're playing with big power and anything can happen. When you see a race buggy driver fully kitted-out nowadays, ready to race in all weathers, they may have as many as 50 different extra accessories on top of the essential kite and buggy.

Essentials:

- Crash helmet protects from hitting other objects or being hit by the board or buggy.
- Strong shoes: your feet take a lot of wear and tear.
- Knee, elbow and wrist guards, protecting vulnerable joints from knocks and hard landings.
- Suitable eyewear, sunglasses to protect from ultra violet and glare, but for buggy drivers more likely goggles to keep sand and spray out of your eyes.
- Gloves.
- Ground stake for immobilising your kite.
- Safety leash (comes as standard with all Flexifoil quad line kites).

Optional:

- Waterproof clothing, some kind of a spray suit.
- Thermal inner clothing.
- Face guard to protect from spray (fits onto the helmet).
- Scarf to protect from spray.

Both the latter can help prevent some of the nasty skin infections you pick up from 'dirty' coastal sites.

- Ankle straps with a ground stake sheath.
- Wind meter.
- Harness – invaluable if you want to board or buggy for long periods and/or in really big winds. You should not consider trying a harness until you have fully mastered the basic elements of kite landboarding or buggying.

- Large ground stake (dog stake or other) for keeping several different sized kites immobilised but ready to fly at one time on days of changeable winds.
- Line equaliser for quick testing if your flying lines are properly equal and by how much they are out if not.
- Line cutter, in case all other safety options fail.
- Chest protector.
- Shin guards.
- Beach tent or cabana to store spare equipment in and to get out of the wind for a rest when you can't take your vehicle onto the beach.

And for buggy drivers in particular:

- Foot peg straps, which will help stop your feet 'bouncing' off the pegs as you go over bumps or steer hard through turns.
- A speedometer so you know how fast you're going.
- A compass to know which direction.
- A watch to know how long you've been out.
- Rear kit bag to carry spare kite, lines, handles, emergency food and drink.
- Extra wide soft sand tyres.
- Extra wide axle to reduce sideways skid.
- Buggy belt to strap yourself in for some jumps on the sand dunes or simply to hold you in under extreme power (this can be extremely dangerous).

- Tandem kit for attaching another buggy to the rear of your buggy (there is theoretically no limit to how many buggies could be attached in a 'tandem').
- Teflon based lubricant (bike chain spray) for maintenance of the bearings.

3. SNOWKITING

"The big difference is that you're riding in 3D, like an Alpine Tony Hawkes. Ram Air kites are highly recommended, with a 10 m² you should be able to ride 90% of the time. But watch out for crashing: hard contact with our planet hurts a lot more up in the mountains than on the water."

Jerome Josserand, Flexifoil International team snowkiter

Snowkiting is a sport which, considering its apparently enormous potential, had until relatively recently failed to inspire much interest compared with buggying and kiteboarding. The huge surge of popularity in all forms of traction kiting during the last five years has given snowkiting its chance to emerge into the public gaze and awareness. In fact, given the slowness with which the medium had been exploited, arguably the fastest progress is currently being made by the snowkite tribe. It's a sport very much on the verge of coming of age.

As it stands now, there is an established snowkite world championship tour, visiting spots all over Europe, with growing numbers of snowkite centres in many countries, which are helping give the scene its momentum in terms of market growth, R&D, equipment development, skill levels and exposure, raising awareness and encouraging new people into the sport. Competitions tend to take one of two possible formats: freestyle (similar to kiteboard freestyle) and racing. Freestyle is all about tricks, transitions, big airs and fluid riding. Racing is quite simply fastest rider from A to B. With the growth in market similar to that experienced by kiteboarding a couple of years ago, manufacturers have been encouraged to design specific snowkite equipment (boards, kites, etc.) knowing that the sales volumes they need to make such projects viable are now achievable.

There are three kites in the Flexifoil quad line ram air range that are recommended for snowkiting. It's also technically possible to use the Fusion and Ion inflatable kites on snow, they've been tried and have worked, as have many inflatable kite designs. Those kites were designed for water use though and we would advise against it. You would be better off to learn snowkiting with a ram air kite, giving you a distinct safety advantage, particularly launch and land autonomy. And do you actually need water re-launch capability? All Flexifoil's high performance ram air kites can be used for snowkiting, but only one – the **Sabre** – was specifically designed for the purpose. Medium aspect ratio kites are the best choice for beginner snowkiters, being very stable, less strong-pulling and medium speed. High aspect ratio kites are more suited to experienced riders, having more aggressive pull, faster speed and faster turns, great for faster, harder carving, jumps and more complex transitions. The Sabre, with its de-power system and cross bridle pulley steering, combines the best features of both.

The snowkite scene is really buzzing nowadays but actually there's nothing all that new about it. Back in the 70s, around the time Merry and Jones were developing their Flexifoil concept, two Swiss skiers, Andreas Khun and Dieter Strasila, were experimenting with a rudimentary version of snowkite, using old parachutes bought secondhand from NASA, mainly to see if they could be used to access ski spots not served by the ski lifts. They called it paraskiing. Later they switched to paragliders, which gave them the added bonus of paragliding back down or, better still, flying in and out of an isolated spot on a paraglider, which could also double as their kite for paraski. That's probably one reason why a number of paraglider manufacturers have now got involved in manufacturing ram air kites for snowkiting and other traction activities. Ram air kites have been the most popular choice for snowkiting, largely because of their extra manoeuvrability and the autonomy factor (you don't actually need a helper for the launch and landing phases). But increasing numbers of inflatable or tube (see 'Water Kite' section) are being seen on the snow, some being designed specifically for snowkiting. They've brought with them principles such as de-power and quick release systems which have now been incorporated into ram air kite design.

It's taken almost 30 years for Khun and Strasila's idea to really happen but nowadays there are increasingly large numbers of riders on the snow each winter, using ever more sophisticated equipment. And the skill levels have developed enormously with it. Riders are trying many of the powered-up water freestyle tricks and huge jumps. But remember, although snow is just frozen water it is a good deal harder and less forgiving. There's a risk of serious injury, those associated with both skiing and power kiting. Always ride safely and use appropriate safety leashes and other devices where these are fitted.

There's a lot of attraction in snowkiting as a great winter alternative to kiteboarding, if you aren't lucky enough to have the kind of lifestyle that allows you to go south chasing the sun every winter. Although Britain isn't a top alpine sports destination, nearby mainland Europe generally is quite well blessed with snow-covered adventure playgrounds in the Alps, Pyrenees, Dolomites, Scandinavia etc. Be aware, however, that you can't just turn up at Tignes and get out on the slopes. It may be more difficult to snowkite there because of the increased risks of and to the large numbers of leisure skiers and boarders. Most 'recognised' ski stations and spots actually prohibit snowkiting for exactly those reasons. But there are increasing numbers of

authorised spots around and lots of virgin space where snowkite is very much allowed and very much on the increase.

If you do get into snowkiting you will need to develop three sets of skills to be able to ride safely. Kite skills, board or ski skills and, most importantly, you will need to develop the skill of understanding the mountains and snow. The risks are enormous, specially off piste which is where most snowkiters will be… Risk of avalanche or of falling badly,

but also the risk of the weather closing in to cut off your route or simply losing yourself in the wide open spaces. And that's all in addition to the normal risks presented by the flying of large traction kites and the wearing of skis / snowboards. You will need to be well protected and well prepared. That means crash helmets, harness, warm clothing, goggles, gloves etc. but also spare kite, food, drink, map, ice axe, mobile phone, some kind of GPS an avalanche rescue device, etc.

On snow, as on water, you can choose to ride with independent handles (if it's a ram air.) or with a control bar. The same arguments apply as before. Using handles gives you greater mobility and manoeuvrability of the kite, using the control bar is simpler with

▲ Snowkiting can be done on board or, as here, skis

the possibility for having a de-power system and performing hands-free manoeuvres such as 'grabbed' jumps. The vast majority of riders use a control bar. If you already have a kite and are thinking of moving into snowkiting it's a good idea to check with your local dealer or the manufacturer whether your kite is suitable, or whether you

should consider something more adapted to snowkiting.

The ideal spot for learning snowkite is a wide-open flat, expanse where the wind may be smoothest. Frozen lakes usually offer the best opportunities as these can extend for vast distances. If you're snowkiting in the mountains at altitude, be aware that the air is thinner and you may need more wind or a bigger kite to get the power you want, but watch out for wind surges and sudden changes in conditions! Generally speaking the friction on snow and ice is much less than on water and the power required to get moving is consequently at least one kite size less than you would need for water. You'll need to decide whether you want to ride a snowboard or with skis. The snowboard's similarity to a twin tip kiteboard makes it a good choice for winter kiteboarders, whereas people already into skis may well wish to stick with them. General opinion is that it's actually slightly easier to learn on skis because you retain independent movement of your feet.

Learn the basics without using a harness, flying smaller kites to begin with, before you try attaching yourself to a bigger kite with much more power. Again, the best thing would be to go to a school and do a course; as usual it will accelerate your learning process. At present the best place to look for school contacts is in the kiteboard and power kite magazines or on the internet, just type 'snowkite schools' into your search engine.

GETTING STARTED AND GETTING UPWIND

If you've already had a go at landboarding, buggying or kiteboarding then the basic principles won't be at all strange, other than the new medium. The method of generating power or traction with the kite is the same and for beginners there's a simple test you can do to determine which is the correct kite size. Launch your kite, put it at the zenith and if you can't walk backwards holding the kite there it's too big. Change down a size. Avoid going out over-powered. Inland wind, specially in the mountains, can be very gusty and changeable. If you're ripped out by a gust it could well mean the end of your session, day or even holiday. And don't overestimate your ability, try to be honest, you'll learn quicker. Finally, whether you're using a control bar or handles, a board or skis, always, always attach your safety leash(es).

Establish a safe area downwind of at least two line lengths. Unroll your kite and either weight it down along the trailing edge (in moderate winds) or the upwind tip (stronger winds) with snow, as described using sand for weight in the Quad Line Kites chapter. In stronger winds you should set up near the edge of the wind window. If you're flying with handles, re-wind about four or five turns of the brake lines onto the handles, if you're on a control bar pull the rear lines in as far as the stop, both of which actions will

▶ Kite locked in position for a long, sweeping run

fully action the brake lines and prevent the kite self-launching. When you're properly ready to launch, let out the brake lines and slowly move backwards until the front of the kite starts to lift up and the kite inflate with air (or the downwind tip if using the strong wind method). Pause at this point and allow the kite to inflate as much as possible before take off. You can launch the kite exactly the same way as described earlier in the book, allowing for yourself to be pulled some way forwards as the kite passes through the power zone of the window on its way up

to the zenith. Don't forget to de-power your Sabre (or grab and pull the trim adjustor) to allow it to climb and to minimize lateral pull in the power area. That means already having your kite hooked in. Kites without de-power systems should be launched before hooking in.

Learning to launch from and use the edge of the window will be very important when it comes to dealing with stronger conditions and riding out wind surges. If you are using a non-depower kite, now is the time to hook in, before you get your skis or board on. Don't

take your eyes off the kite for more than second at a time. Be methodical about setting up and you'll avoid endless to-ing and fro-ing untwisting lines etc. Try some test launches and landings before you get onto your board or skis to make sure everything's ok.

As usual you get yourself going slightly downwind before you start trying to work the edges of your skis or board and the kite position to hold a line across the wind, the ultimate aim of the learning phase in all power kite sports. Position your board or skis accordingly, pointing at 45 degrees downwind, to your 'good' side. Step in to the bindings upwind foot first, making your own decision whether to approach from behind or in front of the board or skis (see Landboarding section for advantages and disadvantages). When you're sure you're ready and the kite is stable…

- Bring the kite slightly back in the wind window, then dive it down in front of you but not too low, just enough to power it up, then towards the edge of the window you're facing towards (your direction of travel) to get you moving forwards. Be careful not to let the lines go slack, or the kite will fold up and fall down the window, then pick up again viciously as the wind kicks back in. Try to start leaning back and working the rear edges of your skis or board with heel pressure to create resistance and keep the line tension.

- Once you've stabilised everything you can begin to work the kite in that small 'S' pattern, remembering to sheet out your Sabre control bar to help the kite climb, gradually working the edge of your board or skis more, too. Once you've got some speed up, the apparent wind factor will begin to apply and you may be able to 'lock' the kite in position towards the edge of the window with constant power.

- While building the power in the kite you should also be trying to work the edges of your skis or board further and further round until you hit your 'reach' line, across the wind. Watch out for the apparent wind factor and be ready to work or de-power your kite to avoid overpowering.

It all comes down to good synchronisation of these basic elements: holding a good line with your skis or board, acceleration and speed. At all costs avoid taking the kite behind you towards the rear of the wind window as this will almost certainly lead to an uncomfortable wipe out. Without a doubt your first few runs will take you downwind but with practice you will be able to hold a line and eventually get back upwind. That means learning how to work the kite and your skis or board together to hold the upwind line, avoiding the lateral apparent wind effect and gradually regaining the ground you may have lost, for instance, while turning round or jumping… With such low friction you can keep the kite relatively high to avoid lateral over-powering but low enough to be able to work the edges.

◀ No more waiting for the ski lifts

STOPPING

Across or downwind, there's also no doubt that at some stage you're going to need to slow down and/or stop without hurting yourself, preferably learning how to turn 180 degrees so you can make your return run back to your start point. Unless you skipped the earlier sections on landboarding and buggying, you'll already have guessed roughly what's involved in all these manoeuvres seeing as what we're basically doing is translating the same wind factors, kite and board skills from one activity to another. To slow down and stop:

- Dig your rear edge(s) in with heel pressure to turn slightly upwind.

- At the same time manoeuvre your kite up the edge of the wind window towards the zenith but still facing slightly towards your direction of travel. Again, be careful not to take the kite behind you with any power.

- As the kite de-powers near the zenith you will gradually come to a stop. Pay careful attention to the kite at this point to make sure it doesn't power up again unexpectedly. Either step out of your bindings or choose a new direction of travel and set off again, avoid spending time in your bindings with the kite flying but not going anywhere.

That's the beginner, low-speed version, which of course you'll need to be able to do going

▶ Excellent view of the de-power system (he's sheeting in for extra jump power)

both. ways, so make sure practise both. You will also be able, with practice and experience, to make faster, more aggressive stops by keeping more power in the kite, moving and then de-powering it quicker, and edging harder. But as with snowkiting generally, you should avoid powering up too much, and certainly too soon. Always stop and get out of your ski or board bindings before attempting to land your kite, with or without helper. And don't forget that if you're using an appropriate kite safety leash, you can always release the kite as an emergency stopping measure. And to do so safely you will need to practise releasing and recovering, off and on skis or board.

TURNING ROUND

The 180 degree turn, which you will need to get back to your start point, is a combination of all the elements you would expect if you've already done any skiing or boarding and had some power kite experience, or read the earlier sections of this book. If you're a snowboarder there's no problem, you're riding a twin tip that can go backwards and forwards like a four-wheeled landboard. That way you can stay in the more natural position, riding backside, leaning back, working the upwind edge into the snow. It's exactly the same manoeuvre with the kite as with the landboard, up the window to the zenith

(careful not to let it get behind you), slow down to a stop and power up going back the other way, leading with your other foot. The same frontside option applies as does to the landboard though, meaning you could choose to turn more like a skier, actually shifting your weight and balance to the other edge, turning round to lead with the same foot, now on the frontside edge but flying 'blind' over your leading shoulder. For a snowboarder, slalom is a series of back and frontside edge turns.

As a beginner, carving round through 180 degrees on snow should always be done downwind. The turn is initiated with the board or skis and you will need to try and drive through the turn smoothly and as fast as manageable to avoid de-winding the kite. Likewise, try not to turn too wide for the same reason, going in with reasonable but not excessive power and powering up sufficiently quickly afterwards for you and the kite to get round comfortably.

■ Initiate the move with your board or skis by gradually bringing them flat and adopting a more upright body position, weight moving over towards the downwind edge of your board or skis, at the same time steering the kite up the wind window towards the zenith

■ With the kite at the zenith there will be a moment when you are flat on the skis / board pointing downwind. Keep driving through the turn to avoid de-winding the kite, quickly bring your weight over the opposite edge of your skis to the one you were on at the frontside edge of your board

◀ Perfect body position for board snowkiting

- Power the kite up again by diving it slightly into the power zone and bringing it over towards the edge of the window you now wish to move towards, working the edge(s) of your skis or board with heel / toe pressure to complete the turn.

- As you come out of the turn on skis you will have executed a foot shuffle so as to be leading with your other, upwind foot, flying front on to the kite and leaning back against the pull in the 'natural' position. On a snowboard you will now be riding on your toes, still leading with your good foot, but now leaning forwards and flying the kite over your lead shoulder, not nearly so natural feeling.

Whichever version you've done, with experience you'll find – as you may already have done on skis or board without a kite – that you can 'jump' your board or skis through the turn, helping keep you moving through it. And that you will be able to carve harder, meaning you can keep the kite more powered up which will also help you make a faster, smoother turn.

JUMPING

On snow more than anywhere, you must exercise extreme caution when learning to jump. Snow and ice can be hard enough landing surfaces without the dangers presented by hidden rocks, or catching a gust, over-shooting and landing on rocks or hard frozen ground. Competition

▶ Getting some big air in the mountains

riders have been known to hit jumps of 30 seconds or more duration! Strange things can happen in the mountains with the contours and wind currents when you spend that long airborne. Be very aware of the risks and start with small jumps and relatively low power until you've fully mastered the technique.

The basic technique is the same as for kite landboarding. You're jumping from a cross wind reach and landing travelling in the same direction. That means you'll have some downwind travel while you're airborne so make sure you allow plenty of downwind space to allow for that, plus some more for getting moving again on landing. Remember, yours and other site users' safety is your responsibility. If you're using a control bar fitted with a quick release safety system, hook into it before your jump.

- Increase your speed, building the power in the kite by working it lower and/or pulling your control bar towards you if you have a de-power system. Start edging you board or skis slightly harder to increase resistance and be ready to spring into your jump.

- Move the kite quickly up towards the zenith and centre window, pointing straight upwards, and as you feel the kite beginning to lift you off the ground, release the resistance from your skis or board to spring into the air.

- Use a little front hand pressure on the control bar to keep the kite stable and stop

it drifting towards the rear of the wind window, and keep your board or skis flat to minimise wind drag. As you feel the jump reaching its peak, start moving the kite forwards in the window again and slightly down, powering it up slightly to give you a softer landing. Don't oversteer at this point or you'll have a hard, fast landing.

- Keep the kite high and watch the ground now to spot your landing. Careful not to let your skis cross at this vital point and try to angle skis or board slightly downwind, relatively flat, rear tips slightly before the front tips. Bend your knees and be ready to absorb the landing.
- Once you've landed bring the kite lower to power up and get you moving again, slightly downwind at first, then edging harder with your board or skis to get back onto a cross wind reach and power the kite up again with apparent wind.

You will need good timing and kite and board co-ordination at the critical moments: take off and landing. Time the movement of the kite, releasing your edge and springing with your legs to get you up; time the powering-up of the kite for landing sufficiently early to land gently but not so much that you land hard and fast.

With practice you'll soon be able to ski back and forward across the wind, get upwind, and fully master the basic elements. At that point you'll be ready to try some of those basic jumps, eventually, if all goes well, using the snow contours and wind currents to boost some seriously sick airs. It's strongly recommended that you take a course in snowkiting at an accredited school, specially if you are thinking about taking it to a more serious level. Please make sure that you're fully protected (with clothing and insurance) before you try jumping on snow, accidents can all too easily happen and you may well have a few crashes during the learning phase. Enjoy your snowkiting but most of all, enjoy it safely.

4. KITESKATING AND POWERED BLADING

"The Wheels of Doom ride about 5mph faster than a buggy; you can use a bigger kite and lean harder against its pull to generate more power. I've ridden thousands of miles now and hit speeds of over 55mph!"

Bob Childs, kiteskater, inventor of the Wheels of Doom

Flexifoil manufactures three kites that are suitable for kiteskating, the **Sabre**, **Rage** and **Blade**. Kiteskating and powered blading means low resistance, high speed and hard crashes. This is not one for the faint hearted, full safety equipment is recommended. Mostly done on a kind of landboard version of roller skates or blades, using landboard wheels and a full fitting roller blade style boot. This is another kite traction area where one man has almost single-handedly championed the cause, an American traction freak currently living in Europe, Bob Childs.

Bob Childs is the Cory Roeseler of his sport. He's been kiteskating (his word) since the mid 1980s and, combining the best of Roeseler with the best of Peter Lynn, was the first to devise a workable kiteskate set up. As with Lynn's buggy, Childs' innovation with skates has been much imitated and developed since but the basic format has never been bettered. His 'Wheels of Doom' have been demo-ing at kite and extreme sports events in Europe and America for years and represent for him

a serious commercial concept. Check out the doomwheels website for a more in-depth picture of the kiteskating scene and Bob Childs' leading role in it, plus a superb photo gallery to inspire your learning phase.

One or two other companies now manufacture something vaguely like them and you should try skate and kite retailers as a first suggestion. If you find them difficult to track down you're looking at a DIY project, in which case go back to the doomwheels site where he gives you details of how to do exactly that. If you want to try with conventional roller blades you will find that you need a smooth hard surface like tarmac or concrete. That means fast action and hard crashes and, for that very good reason, off-road style of doomwheels seems the better option.

Blades and skates are a bit more like water skis and wakeboards in so much as you strap yourself in first and then launch the kite to power yourself up. That in itself presents dangers because if you get into difficulty you cannot detach yourself from them, you will have to deal with the kite somehow. Saying that, clearly the potential is there to go very fast with such low resistance and there's more freedom of movement for jumps and tricks than with landboards. Time will tell.

Start with a small kite, sufficient to get you moving. Until you have mastered the basics with a small kite don't attempt it with a bigger one. Even so, being strapped in you don't want to launch the kite in centre window with full power, so you need to set things up carefully. Work out your regular or goofy stance and go in that direction to begin with as you will be leading with one foot. Pick a moderate wind day and, as before, objective one is to learn to ride backwards and forwards across the wind:

- Set up the kite close to the edge of the wind window, on the side to which you want to go.

- Put your blades or skates on along with your other safety equipment and get ready to launch the kite, pointing yourself slightly downwind to help get moving. Your feet should be parallel, with your good foot slightly advanced. Another option would be to launch the kite sitting down then use its pull to lift you once you've got the kite to the next stage…

- Launch and fly the kite straight up the edge to the zenith, balancing your body to lever against any pull. If you move forward a little don't worry, taking the kite to the zenith will slow / stop you again.

- Now, bring the kite slightly back in the wind window, then dive it down into the wind window towards the side you want to move towards. It will begin to power up and you will begin to move forwards. Don't dive too far down or you may find too much lateral pull. You will need to make some body adjustment to lever against the pull. Keep your knees bent, leaning back against the kite.

- You may need to 'work' the kite to keep

▶ Kite traction pioneer Bob Childs on his Wheels of Doom

105

just the right amount of power on, or off! Once you're moving you need to use heel pressure to start steering your blades across the wind, at which point the apparent wind factor will come into play.

As with the other power kite sports, obviously you will make your first runs slowly, with a small kite, before you start powering up more and leaning harder to build up resistance and more apparent wind. Stopping requires similar technique and timing as for the other land based activities and plenty of practice to be able to stop in exactly the place you want…or need !

■ Take the kite up the edge of the wind window towards the zenith, pointing straight up. The kite will be flying to one side of you and will act as a brake. Don't let it get behind you or you risk a heavy fall backwards, take the kite higher in the window to lose power.

■ Turn your skates to point further upwind, so you're flying over your shoulder. You will quickly come to a stop.

■ Keep the kite at the zenith or land it right on the edge of the wind window.

As your skill level improves you'll be able to make those aggressive types of power slide

or stop we've already spoken about in landboarding, buggying etc.

Turning is done the same way as usual, downwind, similar to a buggy, or a snowkiter on skis. Kite up the edge of the wind window, transfer your weight to come upright then lean over onto the other foot to turn the blades; kite across the top of the win dow, transfer your weight to come upright then lean over onto the other foot to turn the blades; kite across the top of the window then down into the power zone on the appropriate side for your new direction of travel. With practice you'll be able to carve tighter, more aggressive turns, the small size and light weight of the skates making it easier to get over onto the other edge. You won't have the restriction that a board rider has of inhibited foot movement. Independent foot movement gives you the freedom to make rapid transitions with your feet while in motion, so that you're leading with your 'good' or 'bad' foot but can always stay face on to the kite. But you'll also have the freedom to choose front or toeside riding if you want.

Likewise jumping, where the kite and riding mechanics are exactly the same as those used on a landboard or on snow. Your landings will be harder though with no board or ski flex to help cushion them. That means all the shock absorbing will be done by your knees and ankles!

We've only touched very lightly on the potential in kiteskating here, largely because that's exactly what power kiting itself has

◀ A control bar makes a great trapeze

done up to now just scratched the surface. It's an under-exploited format as things stand, but as has already been seen in these sports, things don't always stay that way. If all the pioneers had lost their 'try, try, try again' spirit, power kites would never even have got off the ground in the first place. Kiteskating's day may still come, people just need to see the possibility…

5. JUMPING AND BIG AIRS WITH TRICKS

If you get into getting your airs in a big way you'll be looking for two things, distance and hang time. The biggest officially recorded distance jumps have been of well over 100ft/ (30metres) and have been done with the help of full support and back up teams, not to mention medical assistance on hand if necessary. Stories of even bigger training and accidental jumps abound, with varying degrees of amazing escapes, broken bones and sometimes more serious consequences.

You can use big stacks of Flexis or big single traction foils, both will do the job. As we mentioned in the basic jumping section, four line kites may not be a good bet as they are very responsive, ok on the ground but once you're up in the air, the slightest uneven pull on a handle or line could send the kite back into the power zone or collapse it completely. You may prefer to use a control

▶ Handles are easier for front/back rolls

bar which will cut down the kite's responsiveness and help keep it more stable, certainly if you're a snowkiter, land or kiteboarder trying to work out a move, as this will help you simulate the conditions you'll be in on your board.

The basic idea of the tricks is to start actually using your trajectory, momentum and hang time, in the same way that kiteboarders have been doing to such effect, to hit some rotations or other gymnastics. Like everything else try in moderate winds with some smaller airs to begin with. You will be landing on hard ground at speed. Build up in power and size of your jumps gradually as you gain skill and confidence, but be careful as any kite big enough to lift and keep you off the ground for several seconds could also lift you away in a gust or surge, even when 'parked'

in the safe position up at the zenith.

Don't forget, you should concentrate on jumping upwards, the wind speed will take care of forward travel. Get into your jumps exactly as described in the jumping section. If you've read all the preceding sections you'll realise that it's the same basic technique for all the other kite power sports: kite near the edge of the window, build the power up then send the kite quickly up to the zenith. Hey presto!

Single and multiple rotations in a horizontal axis are the best starting point. As you leave the ground, 'throw' your head and shoulders round to lead the rest of your body through the rotation, hopefully with enough air time to get fully round before you reach ground again. If you've been running one way to get leverage for your jump try and use that

momentum to help initiate and drive the rotation. Rotations in the air means rotations in your flying lines, so you'll have to untwist again afterwards, or pre-twist before lift off. The safest way to untwist is to put the kite at the zenith and quickly spin yourself the appropriate way on the ground, being careful of those gusts.

Another possible jump trick is a front or back somersault or roll. Execute your jump as before but this time launch your body forwards or backwards, leading with the head and shoulders, between your flying lines or under your control bar to execute the roll. Be very careful with your feet, try to 'tuck' your legs and keep your feet out of the way of your flying lines as they pass between them. A snagged line could mean a fouled jump and possible heavy crash as a result. Using handles will give you more space to rotate your body, but using a bar will give more of a trapeze to swing from

Be aware that any sizeable jump is going to result in long downwind travel and very heavy landing so you will need good spatial awareness to be able to 'spot' your landings feet first rather than head first. And you really do need to be fully protected with helmet, gloves, strong footwear and elbow, knee and wrist guards. It's very tiring and you won't be able to keep going too long. Specially as all your jumps will be taking you downwind leaving you a stamina-sapping walk back upwind to your launching spot, trying to keep your kite(s) at the zenith with no power.

◀ Body surfing with a stack of Flexis

Whilst acknowledging that you've got to be relatively bonkers to try kite jumping, try even so to take care with getting your airs, just like all your other power kiting disciplines, and minimise the risk to you and others. That way you'll enjoy your power kiting to the max.

6. BODY SURFING AND DRAGGING

All though not strictly something you do on land, it counts as a halfway house activity on the way to kiteboarding and you're going to end up doing some body drag or surf as part of your kiteboarding beginner course should you decide to sign up for one. It's good fun, easy to learn and you don't need a board or buggy. What you will need is a wet suit because dragging your body along through shallow water is just inviting those rocks, razor shells and other flotsam and jetsam to enter where they're not at all welcome. Those of you using four line kites will need your harness, this is a great learning phase for how to let yourself be pulled by the kite, how to power up and de-power and the principle of pushing the bar away from you to help it climb. It's also a good way of getting used to flying and working the kites while in the water.

Any stack of kites or single big kite will do the job and any line configuration, two or four. Water kites are obviously a good idea because if at any stage you drop your kite

▶ Body dragging is a great way to prepare for kiteboarding

in the water you may be literally sunk with a ram air. It's not complicated to do, in fact it's much like skidding on land. You may need-some kind of flotation jacket will help make sure your body is well up in the water if the kites de-powers for any reason.

The best way to body drag is by flying your kite in a figure eight, diving the kite down the middle of the window and up the sides, which is precisely the manoeuvre you need to practice for making your water starts on a kiteboard. That's if you want to go straight downwind, albeit zig-zagging slightly. You can try body dragging across the wind too, if you keep the kite on one side of the window and try flying the figure 'S' up and down that side of the window as described earlier, you

should go further to that side.

Be especially careful when body dragging in coastal water. The safest is a side shore wind, allowing you to go along the shoreline, never getting too far from land and able to leave the water to get back upwind when you need. Avoid off shore winds as these obviously could drag you out to the danger of the open sea.. Light on-shore is ok too, although it will be hard work walking out far enough for a decent drag back in through even shallow water whilst flying a big kite. It's perfectly possible to cross rivers, lakes and reservoirs, depending on their size but you need to be sure you have the skill and strength to get across and a landing spot. And some means of getting back again afterwards with your gear.

WATER KITES

6

"If there's one thing in life you've got to try once, this is it. For me, kiteboarding is the ultimate sport!

JASON FURNESS, FLEXIFOIL INTERNATIONAL TEAM KITEBOARDER AND
FLEXIFOIL INTERNATIONAL KITEBOARD TEAM MANAGER

LEADING EDGE INFLATABLE (LEI) KITES

An Introduction to 'Water Kites'

"The last three years have been amazing. It was always my dream to become World Champion. After winning in 2004 I re-set my goals and I've managed to achieve them again, retaining the title in 2005 and 2006. Having a great set of kites made all the difference. With Flexifoil's support I've been able to perform consistently at my highest level. They're a great company and I'm glad to be part of it."

Aaron Hadlow, Flexifoil International team kiteboarder, PKRA World Champion 2004, 2005, 2006

People have been experimenting with kite power on water for years and the current explosion of interest in this most radical of extreme kite sports is the result of a long and winding journey to arrive where we are now. The potential was obviously there if only the formula could be perfected. People have tried all sorts of systems and of these, Cory Roeseler's 'Kiteski' rig, water skis with a large, framed kite and a motorised winding/recovery/re-launch system flown on a control bar, which was up and

◀ Live the dream; kiteboarding has never been easier or safer

▶ The original kite waterman: Cory Roeseler, Kite-Ski, 1993

running in 1993, was the closest to what we recognise today as kiteboarding. The system worked but was not commercially successful. Ahead of his (and its) time in many ways, although Roeseler, like other water pioneers, is still very much involved with the water kite scene.

Kiteboarding as we understand it today was probably first done successfully in the south of France, on the Mediterranean coast near Montpellier, some time around 1996/1997. From there it was exported, mainly by one man, Manu Bertin, to Hawaii, or more correctly Maui, to where the likes of legendary long board surfer Laird Hamilton, windsurf icon Robby Naish and designer

Don Montague were also interested and trying to make kiteboarding happen. This small group of power kiters and surf freaks used adapted surfboards and the kind of big kites that were about at the time. Those mostly, but with one notable exception, consisted of big ram air kites such as the two line Peels, four line Skytigers and others which quickly followed. From France and Hawaii kiteboarding has now been successfully exported to dozens of countries around the world.

Clearly there was one big issue that had not really cropped up in kiting before to any great extent : water re-launching. A ram air kite is made with big vents along the front, which take in water just as effectively as air.

The ripstop fabric is covered with a water proof coating but, after more than a few minutes lying flat on the water, the whole sail becomes water-logged and impossible to re-launch without gathering it all up, swimming back in, drying it out and starting again. And there was another serious issue to overcome: getting back upwind. Early kiteboarders spent a lot of time carrying their gear back from downwind runs, a combination of not yet having the skill, nor a properly adapted kite or board that would make it possible.

The basic point was that once again, activity was running ahead of product development and people were using what kites (and boards)

were available rather than equipment specifically designed for the job. Ram air kites still have their supporters for water use and in a very light wind there's still very little to beat a big ram air kite. There are now highly sophisticated dedicated water use ram airs with de-power systems and good water re-launch, and they merit serious consideration for any would-be kiteboarder. In general wind conditions, however, there's another system that has swept all before it in both the competitive and commercial senses, filling the podium positions at nearly all the major kiteboarding events in the last few years, with predictable consequences for the market.

Inflatable kites...

In 1984, two French brothers and master-mariners from Brittany, Bruno and Dominique Lagaignoux, patented their system for putting sealed inflatable tube stiffeners in a single skinned sail, that could be flown as a kite on two control lines attached directly to its tips. The inflatable sections rendered the kite effectively unsinkable and therefore water re-launchable. Like all great ideas it was very simple. The original kite, very basic by today's standards, flew, pulled hard, and was, technically speaking, fully water re-launchable. The inflatable tube stiffeners, one along the leading edge and a series of vertical ribs, had a dual function, providing a structure and buoyancy. The Legaignoux brothers tried many kiteboarding experiments themselves over the years but without real success. Finally, more than 10 years later when French pioneer kiteboarders like Manu Bertin and Laurent Ness saw the potential, they started using the kites. Very soon, inflatable kites had been better adapted for kiteboarding and began to dominate the market, particularly when opinion formers from the surf and windsurf industry like Robby Naish and Pete Cabrinha, decided that inflatable kites were the way to make the new sport happen, bought a Legaignoux license and started making kites.

The rest, as they say, is history, as successive manufacturers have jumped into the

◄ Winning combination, Flexifoil kites have won three world titles

inflatable kite market. Despite some good success with the ram air Blade in the early days of the sport, Flexifoil themselves saw the need to start making inflatable kites (their first inflatable, the Storm1 was released in 2002) to stay competitive in kiteboard sports and the market. A decision which has since been more than vindicated! Apart from all other considerations, a combination of good graphics, build quality, detailing and the huge arched shape classic inflatable kites take up in flight make them very impressive and they really look and act the part.

Inflatable kites are increasingly sophisticated, not surprisingly with so many companies working on the same basic system, and almost all inflatable (LEIs – Leading Edge Inflatables – in tech speak) water kites are four or five line, with a built in de-power system, like the one now incorporated on ram air kites such as the Sabre, allowing you to pre-tune your kite and adjust the pull while in motion by changing the angle of attack of the kite against the wind. The kites are designed to make getting back upwind easier and they exist in a range of sizes to deal with differing wind conditions and for different weights and sizes of rider. They tend to be somewhat larger in surface area than equivalent powered ram airs, to compensate for their arched shape and the huge resistance against the water of the small boards riders use nowadays.

The normal conventions of kite design

▶ Wipika, the first commercially available inflatable kites

apply, meaning that 'competition', high performance kites are elongated; they have a high aspect ratio, giving them more power but making them more control sensitive. Beginner inflatable kites tend to have lower aspect ratios and be more rounded in shape, making them slower, more stable and generally easier to handle. The ever larger numbers of new riders coming into kiteboarding plus the development of various different riding styles (jumps, waves, speed, etc.) has recently compelled designers and manufacturers to develop moderate aspect ratio allrounder kites, high performance yet stable, easy and, importantly, versatile. In Flexifoil's case, that means complete beginners can use the same model of kite as the pro team riders and both will be able to get what they want from the kite.

With the inflatable tubes to stiffen them, until recently the kites have had no need of a complex bridle. That's meant a return to the simplicity of flying lines attached directly to the kite wing tips. But kiteboarding is an evolutionary sport and the latest evolution of water kites has seen a re-introduction of bridles to leading edge inflatables. The bridles are not as complex as those on a ram air kite but do hold the sail more open (less arched) and – most importantly – give an instant, massive de-power potential. These new kites are known as 'Bow' (from their shape in flight) or 'Hybrid' (because they combine two previously separate technologies) kites.

Whichever type of inflatable kite you fly, one thing is sure: they are all flown on con-

trol bars incorporating de-power and quick release safety systems. Kiteboarding requires far bigger kites and more power than other kite sports so riders wear harnesses to be able to fly for any length of time. Specific kite harnesses are manufactured to deal with the different kind of loading and rider mobility compared to say, a windsurf harness. Harness loops attached to the control bar carry independent quick release safety systems. That means riders can stay hooked in without worrying, using their de-power systems to control the pull, with full safety in case of difficulty. Nevertheless, there are times when a rider might prefer to be

'unhooked', usually for more mobility, for an advanced move like the Handle Pass for instance.

The big budgets that have gone into developing the latest generation inflatable water kites, the features they incorporate and performance they deliver, have given them a dominance it's hard to ever envisage them losing. Ram air kites played a crucial part in the early development of this sport but these days it's a frustratingly huge struggle for market share against the all-conquering arched inflatables…

▲ Water contours make a great trampoline for spectacular jumps

INFLATABLE KITES
Atom, Ion and Fusion

"The Fusion is very comfortable to use in varied conditions. It's easy to fly, you can 'feel' where it is in the window without looking, it's quick to re-launch from the water and it's got good turn speed."

Kirsty Jones, Flexifoil International team kiteboarder

Being a big player in the kite industry is one thing. Competing with some of the heavyweights from the surf and windsurf industries is quite another. It's a potent mix of past experiences, kites – boards – windsurf, coming together to drive the new sport forwards. All manufacturers, Flexifoil included, have been forced to look to their strengths and the result has been a surge of acceleration in research and development of product of all kinds. The industry as a whole was obliged (by a relatively small number of accidents, but occasionally fatal) to take a long hard look at safety issues. Manufacturers and products weren't fully prepared for the sudden growth there was in the sport, but now they've well and truly caught up. 2003 marked a particular watershed with every recognised kite manufacturer developing and incorporating extra safety features, a 'work-in-progress' that still continues.

Flexifoil water kites incorporate advanced safety features on the control bar. All the individual components have undergone rigorous testing and the control bars feature effective quick release safety systems and a safety leash. It's designed to give maximum safety plus maximum rider mobility so it suits all levels of rider, from beginner to expert. We'll look at the bars and safety systems in more detail in the next section, but you can be sure there's never been a better or safer time to learn to kiteboard.

There are two different principles for defining inflatable kite sail areas. The difference is in the surface area of a kite which, though flat when on the ground deflated - the 'flat sail area', has a deeply arched curve when inflated ready for launch and even more in flight, presenting a different sail area to the wind – the 'projected sail area'. Projected area is a calculation based on the sail area divided by a given, arbitrary factor. Flexifoil prefers the flat sail area system and all their water kite sail areas are given as such. Incidentally, this confusion doesn't happen with ram air kites because they are held almost flat in flight by their bridle structure.

The **Fusion** is the top-of-the-range Flexifoil inflatable kite, versatile and high performance but easy to handle, different 'tunings' suiting different levels and styles of riding. It's an ingenious specialist all-rounder and worthy successor to the separate high aspect ratio Storm and medium aspect ratio Strike kites with which Flexifoil established itself as a player in the inflatable kite market. It's a 'fusion' of the best performance and features of both. It's a 'classic' C-shaped arched kite and comes in five different sizes, ranging from 7 m^2 to 18.5 m^2. The two largest sizes are not recommended for beginners, mainly because until you understand exactly how the kites handle and function, you may put yourself and others at risk if you are caught in a sudden squall or gust while flying a large sized kite.

Flexifoil has two other inflatables to complete its range of water kites. These kites fall into the hybrid category described earlier. That's to say, they have a single skin sail with inflatable battens and leading edge, like the Fusion, but they also have a small bridle

▶ Flexifoil Fusion high performance water kite
▶ Flexifoil water kite designer Henry Rebbeck

attached to the leading edge. The Atom and Ion have been developed from the standard 'Bow' kite concept that appeared in 2005. After considerable analysis of the Bow kite concept, the Flexifoil design team took the positive aspects and worked on improving what were evidently negative aspects of the kites' performance to arrive at the improved Flexifoil version. For instance, by considering an integrated kite and control bar idea rather than one before the other they were able to eliminate the need for pulleys anywhere on the kite or control gear, as had been incorporated on earlier Bow kite designs.

The first Flexifoil hybrid was the **Ion**, which appeared in 2006. It's now gone on to a second generation and has been joined by the **Atom**. Both the Atom and Ion are much flatter in shape, specially at the front of the kite, and moderate aspect ratio, making them very stable and efficient. They incorporate even more effective de-power systems than the Fusion, one of the advantages of hybrid kites. This makes them very good for beginners (who tend to be cautious and want maximum safety), for schools, and more advanced riders looking to try wave riding (you can almost fully de-power the kite in an instant to exploit a wave then power up again to go and find the next one). Both kites combine good power delivery with a light, crisp feel on the control bar and are stable enough for riders to fly by 'feel' rather than constantly keeping an eye on the kite. Excellent de-power gives them an excellent wind range (reducing the number of kites you need) and,

with their super-stable handling, makes them ideal for learning new tricks.

The Atom is Flexifoil's entry-level water kite, one that's very simple to fly, ultra-safe and reasonably priced. It's an ideal kite for kite-boarding schools or for an individual beginner looking for a kite that will help them learn and then progress. The Ion, now in its second generation, is a higher performance kite without being less accessible. It's the ideal kite for wave riding and for learning new tricks when you pass beyond the beginner stage.

The kite sails are all made from tough ripstop polyester sailcloth, more durable and low stretch than nylon, the leading edge and ribs from heavy duty 170 Dacron. The inflatable tubes and bladders are made of polyurethane, and the pockets they fit into from durable polyester laminate. 'Rigid strut' technology connecting the ribs to the front tube gives Flexifoil's kites great strength and consistent aerodynamic flow. The airflow is helped by rigid (carbon fibre) wing tip ribs or battens, which also gives good, consistent turn speed. The kites are built for durability in extreme conditions and are heavily reinforced at all the wear and tear points, notably the leading edge, trailing edge, line attachment points and wing tips. Like the ram air kite ranges, they are designed in such a way that all sizes have similar handling characteristics.

◀ Board-off moves need big air time

On the Fusion, flying lines attach direct to the sail tips, but multiple front and rear control line attachment point options on the kite (knot-head toggles) make it possible to tune the kite to different styles or conditions; more or less power, faster or slower flying speed. The attachments are necessarily simpler on the Ion and Atom since they offer greater tuning potential via the de-power system but there are nevertheless two attachment toggle options to help you tune your kite to suit your level and style. The kites are designed to ride out wind turbulence and gusts, every inch of the sail studied to help maximise efficiency and reduce drag. They're the product of more than five years of development, designed and built specifically for kiteboarding at its safest and most efficient as the sport stands today.

"Flexifoil should start giving their customers free Frequent Fliers Club memberships, because when you ride their kites you spend so much of your time hitting sick jumps, way up in the air."

Sander Lenten, Flexifoil International
team kiteboarder

Some kiteboard schools take you through a two line kite flying induction before you start dealing with the extra pair of lines and the de-power system. Indeed, some water kites can be flown on two lines and one

▶ A great view of the classic inflatable kite arched 'C' shape

argument two line riders use in their favour is that it forces you to be a better kite flyer, the kites are less forgiving and that makes you safer, you can't rely on something you haven't got (de-power system) to get you out of trouble. Maybe so, but the vast majority of riders nowadays – beginners included – are using four if not five lines. It's also true that if you're used to a conventional two or four line kite, then flying an inflatable kite on four lines with a de-power system changes the whole nature of how you handle the kite, in one very important way, one we described earlier when talking about the Sabre.

With a 'conventional' kite, if you want to generate more power or get the kite to climb, you pull back with your arms and/or walk backwards on the ground. Forget all that. With a de-power system hooked onto your harness, to get the kite to climb you push the control bar forwards, away from you, with your arms, opening the trailing edge, de-powering the kite but enabling it to generate lift from the airflow across its surface. It makes many aspects of handling the kite different and makes it vitally important that you fully familiarise yourself with the kite and de-power system on land before you go anywhere near water. It goes against everything you've learned before and you may need to un-learn old habits as much as learn new ones.

Before we move on, there's another, even more recent safety system development we should mention that we'll be explaining later on in this chapter, the 5th line system. The 5th line system gives riders more autonomy as it means you can safely solo land and re-launch an inflatable kite. It also helps tune the kite to further extend its wind range and upwind performance. It's another feature that has helped make kiteboarding even safer, less intimidating to learn and more user-friendly than ever.

THE AXIS CONTROL BAR, ION AND ATOM CONTROL BAR, DE-POWER SYSTEM, QUICK RELEASE SAFETY SYSTEMS AND 5TH LINE SYSTEM

Flexifoil's latest generation control bar, the Axis Bar, contains all the very latest kiteboarding features. It's a 50cm carbon fibre bar with colour coded bar ends to avoid line connection mistakes and to make correct recovery easier whenever you have to let go of it for any reason. The tip mouldings are stiffened on the inside to allow direct turning control, soft on the outside to protect the rider from contact during tricks etc. There's an ultra-grip hand grip to help maintain control, and for riding powered up and un-hooked when you're at advanced level. The control line line-leaders are pre-attached to the tips and centre. Both front lines attach to the single centre line leader. The rear lines (the 'steering'

lines) attach to the control bar tips. There's one harness loop for hooking into your harness. This carries the de-power system and is usually referred to as the de-power loop or chicken loop. It also carries the primary and secondary safety release systems. The secondary safety system is attached to a leash, connecting the chicken loop to one of the rear line leader lines. There's a swivel incorporated into the leader line for the front control lines. This is to prevent the lines twisting when you loop the kite, and to reduce wear and tear on them.

The Ion / Atom control bars are different from the Axis bar. They were designed for riders looking for easy-to-use gear without compromising performance or the ability to try the latest tricks. The results are simple but effective designs with an adaptable safety system depending on your style or skill level. No pulleys means there's less possibility of tangling your control lines, especially when the kite and bar are down in the water. These bars also benefit from a number of developments first incorporated on the Axis bar. The bars have thermoformed EVA foam grips and ergonomic bar ends. They incorporate a simple but highly effective primary safety release and an efficient de-power system. And there's that stainless steel swivel to keep your centre lines twist-free, a major plus for any control bar, especially one held by a beginner.

THE DE-POWER SYSTEM

"The de-power system is one of the best developments in kiteboarding equipment. With this system, sailing is much less physical, specially in those uneven winds we get in Britain ! With the de-power system kiteboarding has become a true sport for all."

Kirsty Jones, Flexifoil International team kiteboarder

The Axis Bar and the Ion / Atom bars are fitted as standard with a highly effective variable power (de-power) system that is simple to operate. Using the de-power system means using your harness. When you first start flying hooked into your harness on your 'chicken loop' it will feel strange to begin with but you will find everything reasonably straightforward to adjust to.

The heavy-duty, vinyl-coated de-power loop is fitted onto the end of the leader line for the kite's front lines which passes through a fitting mounted at the centre of the control bar. It's universally known as the 'chicken' loop, the inference being that if you need to de-power you must be scared (chicken). Further along this leader line, going away from the bar towards the line attachment points, there's a 'stop' fixed in position. Once you are hooked in, you can regulate the power by pushing the bar away from you (sheeting out) towards the stop, evenly with both hands. With the front lines fixed to your harness via the chicken loop, this has the effect of pushing the rear lines away, breaking the profile of the trailing edge, changing the angle off attack, spilling some of the kite's wind and reducing power. Conversely you'll be able to crank the power up when required by pulling the bar towards you, closing the sail's trailing edge so it's flatter on to the wind.

With skill and practice you will be able to fine-tune the power at various points of your kiteboarding activity, for instance powering up for jumps, de-powering before landing or to surf a wave. Equally valuably, it enables you to deal with big gusts and squalls out on the water, limiting the power surge and hopefully giving you the breathing space you need to ride it out and wait for the power to drop again. In fact, any time you feel that the power is too much and you're hooked into your de-power loop you can use it in this way. Likewise, if the wind drops a little you may be able to keep riding by powering up as far as possible.

There's a second level of power tuning on Flexifoil water kites, which also operates from the control bar. Between the safety quick release and the line attachment point on the centre (front) lines is a 'pull-strap' adjustment system which enables you to 'lock' / tune the whole de-power system and rig at various power settings, varying the range of your de-power. Better still, it can be adjusted either before sailing or in motion, out on the water. To operate it, if you pull the red adjustment toggle it will shorten the front lines, opening the trailing edge and reducing power

▶ Flexifoil water kite control bar showing de-power and quick release systems

(i.e. pull red if in danger). By pulling the blue toggle you lengthen the front lines / shorten the rear lines in relation, thereby closing the trailing edge and increasing the power setting. In either case, releasing the adjustment toggle at the appropriate point 'locks' your tuning. You can make further pre-sailing fine tuning by trying the extra knots on the rear line leader lines attached to the control bar.

In extreme circumstances, if you let go of the bar altogether it will slide along the leader line until it meets the de-power 'stop'. This releases the rear lines and keeps the front lines pulled. What normally happens is that the kite almost completely de-powers and flies itself to the edge or top of the wind window where you can recover it. This is done by pulling on the centre line until the control bar comes back in reach. Get plenty of practice on dry land with your de-power system, trying it in every conceivable circumstance, before you find yourself trying to work out how to do it out on the water.

Please be aware that if you're flying a four line ram air kite on handles or a two line kite on a control bar, you will not have an effective de-power system. In the former scenario you will have the handles to make adjustments to the angle of attack of the kite and, if it all gets too much, a wrist leash for safety (see below).

THE SAFETY SYSTEM

"This bar is super versatile. Our world champion rider Aaron Hadlow has been supplying the R&D team with endless feedback. Our original spinning leash safety system was a first and the new, improved Axis bar system is even more rider-friendly. Not only that, Flexi bars are bullet proof and built to last!"

Jason Furness, Flexifoil International team kiteboarder, Flexifoil International kiteboard team manager

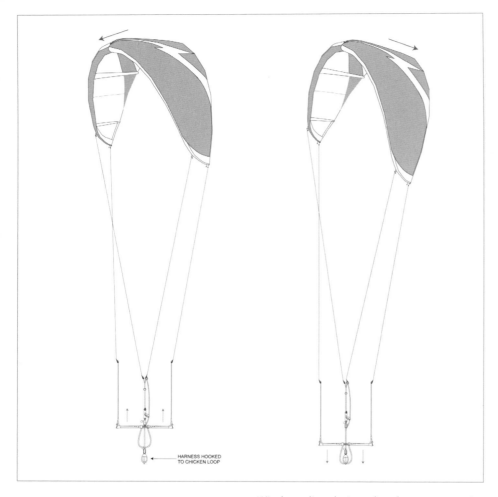

HARNESS HOOKED
TO CHICKEN LOOP

Gordt Foundation was subsequently created to spread the safety message around the kiteboarding world, with Flexifoil team rider Andreya Wharry leading a record-breaking 70 mile, fund-raising crossing from the Scilly Isles to her home spot at Watergate Bay in Cornwall during 2004 (a record she's subsequently beaten). All very conscientious.

But let's be clear about this now, the majority of accidents, fatal or otherwise, happen **before** or **after** the victim is on the water. Without and even sometimes with an effective safety system, sudden big squalls or gusts of wind when you're flying the kite on the beach can easily whip you away and crash you against the nearest fixed object : piers, sea walls, buildings, posts, vehicles…

The first Flexifoil water kites, like their contemporaries, came with a working safety system but it required a leash running from your wrist or harness to one of the (rear) lines. The problem being that for advanced level riders doing jumps and transitions involving full loops or rotations, that kind of leash gets in the way, impedes mobility and can foul rider, flying lines or board, making things potentially much more dangerous. Control gear design has evolved as fast as the kites, in Flexifoil's case resulting in the latest versions, the Axis and Ion Atom bars, which use a spinning leash system that avoids the fouling problems of the early leashes while maintaining full safety for the rider.

The control bar release systems are linked

Kiteboarding being the dangerous activity that it is, safety very quickly became an issue. The death of talented German competition rider Silke Gordt in what most people agreed were avoidable circumstances provoked considerable soul-searching across the industry. The Silke

to the chicken loop and you'll need to be hooked in to be able to make full use of the safety features. As a first step you can let go completely of the control bar which will slide up to its de-power stop, de-powering the kite. If this is not sufficient, you'll find the primary safety release between the chicken loop and the control bar. It's a fluted plastic tube, widening out to form a flat brim at the end. Wrap your hand round it and push hard away from you pushing against the brim. The front lines leader line is now totally released, along with the control bar, releasing the leading edge of the kite, spilling all its wind and retaining it by one rear line and the safety leash. The kite will sink to the ground / water with no power. The primary release system is designed as a re-ride system. You will now need to recover the control bar and the released part of the safety system, re-set the system and re-launch, but that should be possible even on the water. But any safety system is only as good as the person using it (and setting it). Make sure you know how to action and re-set your safety system properly before serious use or going anywhere near the water. Practice using the system in shallow water until you're 100% confident the actions are instinctive, rather than find yourself way off shore, in deep water, unsure of what to do. Don't become another tragic statistic, it's your own life we're talking about here as

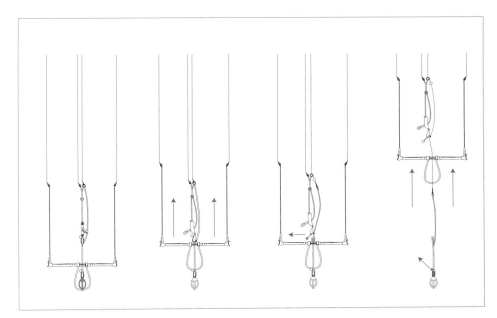

▶ Activating the primary safety release system

well as other peoples'. Follow the manufacturer's step by step instructions and if you are in any doubt, contact your dealer or Flexifoil direct.

As a third level of safety, the bar also has a secondary quick release on the chicken loop itself. This is your ultimate sanction and might be needed if, for instance, a kite you've already let go to this stage is then snagged by a boat propeller. Up to this point you are still attached to the kite and can recover it without too much trouble. Actioning this third, ultimate, safety system completely detaches you from the kite and really should only be used in the most extreme of circumstances. You're safely away from trouble but your released

kite now represents a danger to other kiteboarders or site users. Now you will have to hope that your kite blows to shore nearby or that someone else helps you recover it in a boat. Remember, your safety system will only work if you are hooked into your chicken loop. But the Flexifoil system means you can go for radical, maximum danger moves hooked in.

5TH LINE SYSTEM

You can now buy Flexifoil water kites with either a 4 or 5 line configuration. If you start(ed) with a 4 line bar you can convert it to 5th line flying with a conversion kit available from Flexifoil. The principle of the

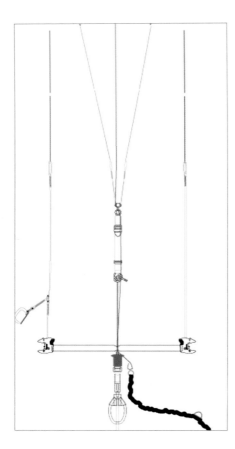

5th line system was developed during 2003 by French kiteboarder and inventor Michel Bousquet. It was clear his system worked, with one manufacturer using it on their kites in 2004, then virtually all the rest, including

▲ The 5th line system has increased rider safety and autonomy

Flexifoil, developing their own 5th line application, which became generally available during the 2005 season.

It was originally conceived as a safe way of completely neutralising the kite in case of emergency. In doing so it also had the effect of 'landing' the kite in a neutral position in almost any wind conditions. And it's a tangle-free re-ride safety system (unlike some previous 4 line safety systems) allowing re-launch as soon as you've recovered your control bar, there's no re-setting to do. The device was first seen in public at the 2004 Mondial du Vent kiteboarding event in France where winds regularly hit 40 knots. Without fail, the system safely landed the kite from any position in the wind window. Not only that, it also enabled flyers of almost any skill level to re-launch their kites – from water and land without needing a huge amount of technique, as had been required up until then.

As other minds have got to work on the principle, it's been adapted to serve an additional purpose, that of an extra kite tuning device. Depending on how you tune your 5th Line, and the Flexifoil system gives you three possible 'settings', it can help in a number of different ways : to give your kite more de-power range, smaller movements of the control bar having greater effect on the kite; lightening your kite steering whilst retaining direct and responsive feel; reducing the edging force required on your board to work the kite closer to the edge of the wind window, in

turn improving kite performance in strong, gusty winds ; improving your upwind performance because the kite is sitting closer to the window edge.

The 5th line connects, at the rider end, to the safety leash, normally attached to your harness. It then passes through the centre of your control bar along with the leader line for your front flying lines. It runs alongside the leader line to the point where the front lines attach, then continues straight to the kite, where it attaches to another, short leader line, itself attached to two toggles fixed to sewn in tabs on the leading edge, forming a 'Y' shape. It's this short leader line at the kite end that has the three tuning options in the form of three knot heads. You attach to different knots heads to achieve different performance tunings, details of which are given in the special 5th Line manual. It's important that you correctly install your 5th line, paying special attention to getting the length exactly right. Incorrect length will deform the kite, impairing its performance and preventing the 5th line from functioning as it should.

As a safety system it's very easy to activate, one that functions when riding unhooked too. In fact you need to unhook, then simply let go of your control bar, which flies away from you but stays on the 5th line. The kite is held by the 5th line only, attached to the centre of the leading edge and your safety leash, so it de-powers immediately, turns onto its back and floats gently to the ground or water. When it lands there will be

no pull or power on the 5th line. This means you can loop it round your board, bury the board in the sand and run to the kite to immobilise it. Or, to re-launch, pull the 5th line in until you can recover the control bar and hook back in to your chicken loop. Once you've fed the 5th line back through the bar, the kite will roll onto one wingtip, power up and make its own way to the window edge ready for re-launch.

SETTING UP YOUR INFLATABLE KITE

As you'd expect, when you buy a Flexifoil water kite, it comes in a logo-d, heavy duty custom storage bag. This bag is big enough to carry your kite fully deflated and rolled or in a temporary pack-down state, leading edge deflated but ribs/battens inflated. It's not recommended that you leave your rib tubes inflated any length of time (no more than overnight).

Carefully follow (and memorise) the step-by-step instructions in your manual. Try to remember, as you unroll the kite for the first time, how it was rolled to leave the factory so that you can do the same when you pack it away each time. You may want to try this once at home but you're going to need to know the full procedure for when you get out on the beach, lake or river side.

▶ Easy, one-hand control leaves the other hand free for water dragging

 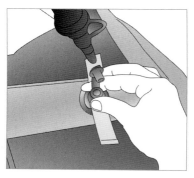 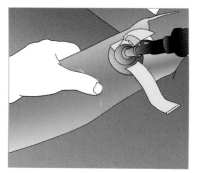 

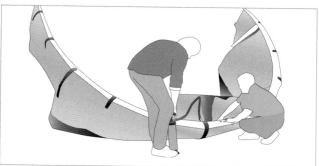 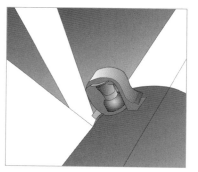 

With the kite set-up and safely immo-bilised, if this was the start of a boarding session, now would be the moment to stop and put on your final pieces of safety equip-ment: crash helmet, harness and buoyancy / flotation aid. You might want to get used to this anyway whilst you're learning to fly the kite as that's the way it's going to be when you come to do it for real. It's a completely different experience flying a big kite with your movement restricted by your wetsuit, harness etc. Specially built kiteboarding wetsuits and harnesses are now produced

▲ How to set up and blow up your kite

and these are designed taking into account the specific ergonomics of extra flexibility of the articulations, along with reinforce-ments in the appropriate places, required by kiteboarders in mind.

The next stage will be to unwind your flying lines. Most riders tend to use lines between 20 and 30 metres long: longer to have a bigger wind window with more space and time to manoeuvre the kite; shorter lines for powered-up fast response and manoeuvrability, say for wave riding. There's a trend among more advanced riders for even shorter lines, as little as 15 metres. This requires advanced flying

technique and is not for the beginner / intermediate rider, ultimately however, it could well provide a way of fitting more riders into less space.

Flexifoil water kites have 20 metre control lines, plus 5 metre extensions you can add as an option. With the 1 metre leader lines on the control bar that means the kite will be a maximum of 26 metres away from you, minimum 21 metres. The lines are made from high performance Dyneema and must be the appropriate strength for the size of your kite and wind range. Unlike ram air traction kites, the lines are all of equal strength as the power is more evenly

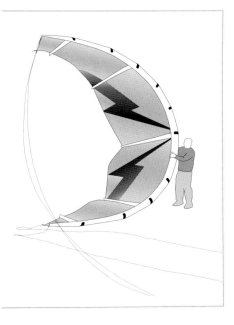

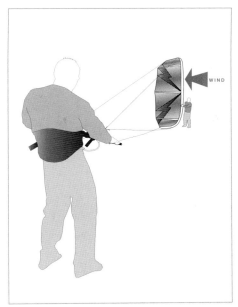

distributed between front and rear. They are sleeved at each end to prevent snapping where knots are tied, and this sleeving is colour coded to help you easily identify the left / right, front / rear lines. The line attachment points on the kite and control gear are also colour coded to prevent incorrect attachment. Attach and unwind the lines as instructed, then double check to make sure they're correctly attached. Then attach your control gear. In principle you will never have to detach the lines from the controls again. Check and re-check that they're all correctly attached and completely free of twists. Launching with lines incorrectly attached

▲ Launch near the edge of the wind window

can put you at risk of serious injury. Ready? I think you probably are…

HOW TO LAUNCH...

Bearing in mind the dangers associated with flying these large kites on dry land, the safest way to launch is with the kite on the edge of the wind window, close to the water. That way, if a big gust hits or you get into difficulties you will be pulled towards the water / away from hard obstacles such as sea walls, fences, etc. As with the other Flexifoil kites, there are two ways of launching an inflatable kite : assisted launch (recommended for beginners) or solo launch (recommended for more experienced fly-

ers only). Even if your kite incorporates a 5th line, for beginners the assisted launch is still advised because until you're used to the manoeuvre there's a chance you could get into difficulties. In big winds and with big kite sizes it's recommended, however much experience you've got, to use the assisted launch. Let's take a look at solo launching first.

Let's assume you're hooked into your harness and in position and so is the kite, on its back lengthways, upwind tip weighted with sand, near the edge of the wind window, leading edge facing the edge of the wind window.

■ Take a couple of paces backwards pulling smoothly, gently and evenly on the control

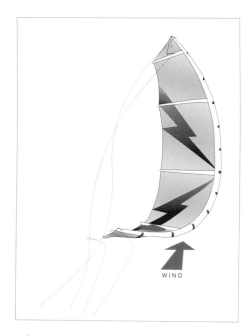

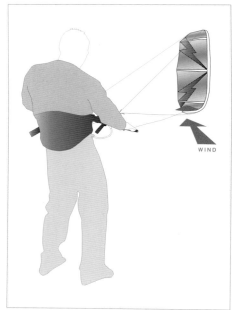

bar. As you do so tension will come onto the downwind tip lines, making the tip rise off the ground. As it does so you will feel pressure beginning to build in the sail.

■ Keep moving gently backwards and the downwind tip will rise further. Then tension will come onto the upwind tip and lines, pulling it towards you. As it does so it will unfold and dump its load of sand on the ground. Hold the bar diagonally, in the same plane as the kite, to help maintain its position facing the edge of the wind window. You will now feel considerably more pressure on the lines as the sail fills with wind.

▲ Solo launching a four line kite at the edge of the wind window

■ Once the kite has got rid of its sand it will lift itself off the ground and as long as you keep even pressure on the flying lines will fly to a 'safe' position on the edge of the wind window.

■ From here you can steer it up the wind window, pulling gently on the upper tip lines while sheeting out with your control bar to help the kite climb, until it reaches the zenith, above your head. Correct your steering to stabilise it there.

For an assisted launch make sure you brief your caddy before you start. It will be preferable to have a more experienced flyer act as caddy at first as they will need to know how to move the kite from its 'immobilised' position to the correct launch position. The caddy

should stand downwind, behind the kite, holding it by its leading edge tube, just below the halfway point, leading edge facing the edge of the window. You will feel the kite pull but, being at the edge of the window, it won't be able to move anywhere. When you're ready to launch, with the kite full of wind and ready to go, they can do one of two thing: on your launch signal they release the kite, take a few steps backwards to get out of the way, and let you fly the your to safety; on your signal to abort the launch, grab it quickly, turn it on its back to de-power it and immobilise it again, leading edge down on the sand, back surface facing the wind. What you must do is to agree your signals. Flexifoil recommends using hand / arm signals because the noise of wind and water can make it difficult to communicate vocally from 30 metres away. It's also important for the caddy to simply release the kite at the appropriate moment, not to try and throw it. Once the kite is out of the caddy's hands you follow the normal procedure for steering it up to the zenith.

STEERING...

With the kite stable at the zenith, this is the moment when, if this was a kiteboarding session, you would get your board leash fastened ready to make your way into the water. Keep checking the kite's position while you do that using one hand to keep the kite steady (hold the control bar near its centre), the other to deal with the board. If you've never flown power kites before, while you're mastering the flying controls, you're advised not to hook in (that's why some schools use small dual line inflatable kites for complete beginners). You need to know how to fly the kite confidently before adding new dimensions such as the harness. If the pull is too much, land the kite and change to a smaller size. If you're not hooked in, at this stage your only way of controlling (as in reducing) power is to move forwards or steer the kite further out of the window. It's going to be a good work out because you'll be dealing with the full power of the kite with your arms then your body, rather than the other way round. If you're hooked in that won't be an issue but you'll need to adjust to letting the power be carried by your body through

the harness point around your waist, and avoiding tensing your arms and shoulders. Try moving the kite backwards and forwards across the top of the wind window at first. The steering is very similar to a two line kite despite the four control lines.

- Pull back gently but firmly on the right side of the control bar at the same time pushing forward with the left, until you see the kite start to turn to the right. As soon as it's pointing slightly to the right, neutralise your steering to let it fly in that direction. It may descend slightly as it does so with the curve of the wind window.

- Before it reaches the edge of the window or gets below halfway down, pull gently but firmly back on the left end of the control bar until you see the kite turn to face slightly left. Neutralise your steering to let it fly back across the top of the window. It will probably rise a little towards centre window and fall again as it moves slightly left.

- Before it reaches the left edge of the window pull back again on the right side and so on. You can stabilise the kite at the zenith again by turning it to point straight up as you reach window centre, then neutralising your steering.

Once you've done that a few times it's time to try some full loops, a manoeuvre that will power the kite up big time as it will come much lower in the wind window and almost certainly drag you forward on the ground, another good reason for being on a smaller sized kite. For those of you flying hooked in, try and remember to sheet out (push the

control bar away from you) to help the kite climb at the appropriate moments.

- With the kite stable at the zenith, pull back firmly on the right tip of the control bar, pushing forward with the left also. It will turn to the right and then continue to turn as long as you keep steering it that way.

- Keep steering it that way and it will turn through 360 degrees, down and to the right, coming round to point straight up the wind window again near window centre. Keep the steering on, even when the kite is pointing straight down and accelerating hard. As it comes round towards window centre the pull will be close to max and you will need to lean back keeping your shoulders well back.

- As the kite comes round full circle and is pointing straight up the wind window, neutralise your steering to allow it to climb up towards the zenith. At this point it will start to decelerate and de-power and you will see the lines are twisted once.

- Just before it reaches the zenith pull back firmly on the left side of the control bar (pushing on the right) to pull the kite into a left hand loop, like you just did to the right. Keep the steering on all the way round until it's pointing straight up and climbing up centre window, neutralise steering and sheet out to help the kite climb.

- At this point your lines are untwisted again and you are ready to start the whole thing again.

The more exaggerated your pull/push with the control bar the tighter the turn.

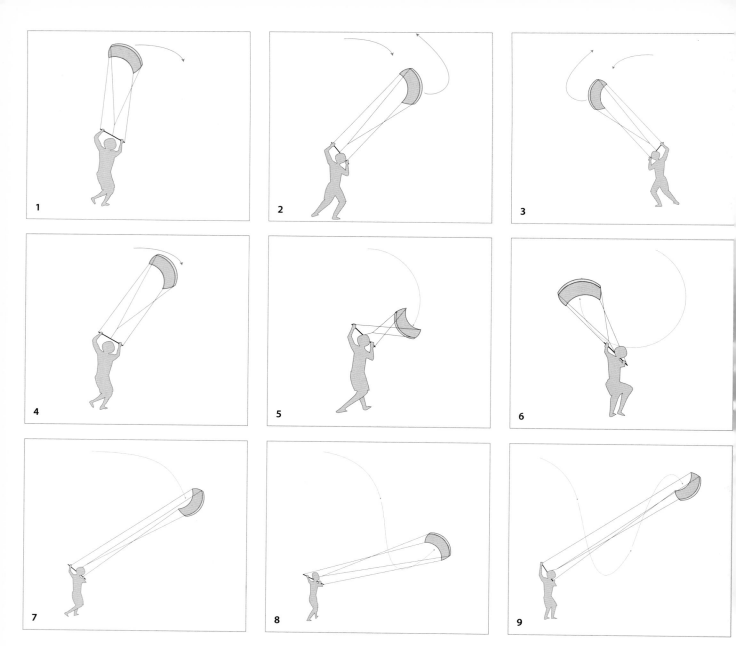

Don't steer too hard at first or the kite may behave unpredictably. Once you're comfortable with that, it's time to try the correct powering-up move for the beach and water starts you're going to be making later on. It's also the basis of the 'S' (sinusoidal) pattern you will need to learn to be able to work your kite to deliver you consistent power.

- With the kite stable at the zenith, pull back gently on the right end of your control bar to move it slightly to the right but still high in the window.

- Now pull back hard on the left side of your control bar to dive the kite down into the window centre at a 45 degree angle. You will feel it quickly power up and accelerate. Lean back! The kite is moving left and it will pull you to the left

- Keep steering down at 45 degrees angle to the ground and as the kite passes halfway down the window on the left hand side, pull back firmly on the right side of your control bar, turning it up at 45 degrees again (a 90 degree turn). Keep the steering on and turn the kite so that it climbs up the left side of the window, sheeting out to help it do so.

- Now reverse your steering to dive the kite down to the left once more, powering up as you dive, then turning up again, keeping the kite on the left side of the window, working it in an 'S' pattern.

◄ 1,2,3 – flying accross the zenith
4,5,6 – full loop of the kite (kiteloop)
7,8,9 – 'S' pattern
▶ Assisted landing at the edge of the wind window

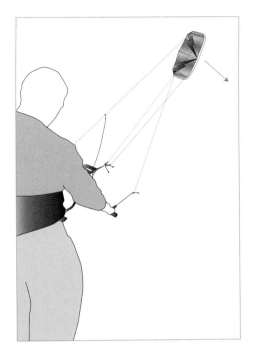

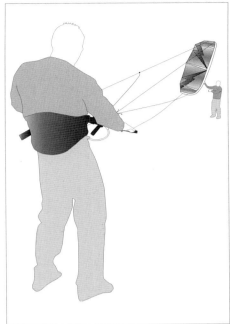

From this point you can keep the kite moving in a continuous pattern, 'working' it up and down the edge of the wind window to try gain power, speed and apparent wind. The lower it comes down the window the more lateral pull there will be (and the more you can work your board's edges when you're on the water). This 'S' is how you'll be able to keep moving in the same direction on your board, to make a nice long run. But that's for later…

LANDING…

As with the launch, the landing is a potentially hazardous moment and your landings should always be made with a fully-briefed helper / caddy. It is not recommended for beginners to solo land and it should not be attempted. If you get into difficulty on dry land and there is nobody available to help, activate one of your safety quick releases to de-power the kite and let it land itself.

First of all you must have a big enough landing area, well away from other site users. If you are in a group of kiteboarders you must agree where is your landing and launching area before starting and always head for there when you want to get off your board and land the kite. You need to have your caddy correctly positioned between 25 and 30 metres downwind of you (depending on

your line length) at the edge of the wind window nearest the water and they should approach the kite from behind, downwind, as you fly it close to the ground.

- With the kite at the zenith, pull gently on the end of your control bar corresponding to the tip of the kite closest to the water. Don't pull it into a full loop, steer it gently but steadily down the edge of the wind window, keeping the leading edge pointing towards the edge of the wind window, never down.

- As the kite approaches ground level, manoeuvre yourself on the ground so you can fly it close to your caddy. Keep flying towards the edge of the window so there's minimum power.

- Your caddy should position themselves so they can approach the kite from downwind, behind it. When your caddy can reach the centre of the leading edge they should grab it, turn the kite on its back and be ready to 'walk' it to a safe position to immobilise it.

- If this was for real, you could now detach your board leash and safety leash and walk the kite to a safe position. Place the kite face down, leading edge on the ground pointing into the wind, and weight the leading edge down with sand to immobilise it.

You should be able to land your kite hooked in or not. If you start with the kite

◀ Original 1998 big volume directional boards
◀ Modern twin-tips are tiny and wafer-thin

at the zenith and fly it down the edge of the window it should have little or no power as it descends.

If you're using a 5th line system, there's a safe way of solo landing your kite which was described a little earlier. You will need to unhook from your harness so it will be a good idea to have the kite somewhere near the edge of the window to avoid having too much pull. Then you simply let go of the control bar. It slides along the 5th line, instantly de-powering the kite and bringing it to land on its back in a neutral position, retained by the 5th line only. If you're not proposing to re-launch straight away it's recommended that you go and turn the kite over to properly immobilise it. You can wrap the 5th line round your board and bury that in the sand to stop the kite blowing away while you do that.

KITEBOARDS

"I would say 90% of kitesurfers are using twin tips. First of all they're easy to use and secondly they suit any kind of conditions. A twin tip is similar to a snowboard, you can ride it in both directions and a big plus is that there's no more need to jibe, compared to a directional where you need to jibe and switch your feet."

Andreya Wharry, Flexifoil team kiteboarder, Extreme Academy kiteboard instructor

▶ Flexifoil team rider Peter Trow smacks one off the lip

In the beginning of kiteboarding, dedicated kite boards didn't exist at all. Most early kiteboarding efforts were made on home-adapted surf or windsurf boards or water skis. All used some kind of foot bindings (like on a windsurf board), essential for working against the pull of the kites. These DIY boards were ok to get the sport up and running but weren't designed for the specific strains and loading of kiteboarding, specially when it came to the issue of jumping, more specifically, the landings after jumps, and the vexed question of getting back upwind.

Of course it didn't take long for shapers and manufacturers from within the established sports of surf, wakeboard and windsurf, specially the latter, to start to look seriously at the new sport and kite specific boards soon started to appear, reinforced for kite power. With its obvious link to windsurfing, most early kiteboards conformed to the directional principle. That is to say, they were made to go in one direction only. They were classic boards with plenty of volume to keep you afloat and a three fin ('Thruster') configuration at the rear for stability, course holding and control. Being mono-directional (forwards only) meant that they had to be turned round for you to get back to your start point, even upwind, skill level, board, kite and conditions allowing. Jibing was as much part of the essen-

tial requirement as water or beach starting and water re-launching. Mainly because the only alternative to jibing was to stop, put the kite at the zenith, take the board off and turn it to point the other way, then water start again…

Just as some kiteboarders came to the sport from windsurfing, so others had had prior experience of wakeboard riding and snowboarding. Wakeboards are generally short and very thin, rider strapped into full foot bindings and towed behind a power boat or jetski, playing and tricking on the boat's wake. Wakeboards made for a much 'trickier' style of riding but being much shorter and less voluminous, riders needed to be super powered-up to stay afloat. Wakeboards, like snowboards, are normally symmetrical lengthways, having fins at both ends to allow riders to lead with either foot during trick sessions. The implication for kiteboarding was immense. Unrestricted by things like masts, the board could be designed to lead in either direction, positioning the rider dead centre, so no more turning round. To go back the other way you simply reverse your direction. The problem with simply using wakeboards was that being so small, fast and radical and needing as much kite power as they do, they weren't really suitable for beginners. Also, that being permanently strapped in to your foot bindings can be very dangerous if you do get into difficulties.

◀ Getting out through the shorebreak, a kite's-eye view

The first twin-tip kite boards were developed by master French rider Franz Olry and started to appear during late 2000, and the first production twin tips during 2001 and 2002. 'Twin Tip' mania was born almost overnight. Kiteboarding had finally established its individuality and different-ness from windsurfing because at the time you couldn't twin tip a windsurf board.

Twin-tips are comparatively small boards – a competition board will be about 120cm long where the old directionals were 2 metres or more! Great for skilled riders but very problematic for beginners. But the development of scaled-up versions suitable for beginners (and bigger sized riders), plus improvements in design and construction over the years in both boards and kites, means it's perfectly possible to learn kitesurfing on a twin tip, cutting out directional boards and the awkward jibe, and not surprisingly this is overwhelmingly the most popular type of board in the world today. Kiteboarding can genuinely claim to be a highly successful fusion of other sports and nowhere is this reflected more than in the rapid evolution of board shaping and design. But the basic kiteboarding board family as things stand today is still directionals, wakeboards and twin tips, plus their 'off-spring': mini twin tips and directionals, mutants and WakeSkates. Directionals have been making a comeback recently as more kiteboarders have tried wave-riding where

▶ Jumping 'unhooked' means big power and hard landings, even on water

the big volume boards are more at home than the 10-metres-up aerial gymnastic riding style. The general principle for all boards is big board small wind, small board big wind. A big volume board in a big wind can be just too much to handle and a small board in a small wind might well sink due to lack of buoyancy or kite power to keep it up.

THE FLEXIFOIL KITEBOARD RANGE

There are three boards in the latest Flexifoil board range. All three are twin tips, not surprisingly, all different sized models of the same basic shape. The board outline has been devised to accommodate different riding styles and not be specific to one style of riding. The boards are made from Airex foam with honeycomb reinforcements under the heelside edge of the board. The result is a board that gives excellent, easy control and a soft ride, handling chop well, an important consideration for less aggressive beginner riders. The boards have great flex, enabling them to become more responsive the harder you ride. The package is completed by ergonomic foot pads and straps and a grab handle on the deckside, plus four 55mm fins on the underside.

The three board sizes start with the 145/42cm (length by width), the biggest size and the best board for bigger sized riders and beginners. Next is the 135/40cm, for lighter sized and intermediate riders. Finally, there's the 130/40cm, the smallest version, suitable

for advanced riders looking for professional performance. The 130 also features a stronger construction and gloss finish and comes with a board bag, is called the Pro model and is more expensive. They're all Flexifoil branded with an excellent five-colour underside graphic. Whichever Flexifoil board you choose you can be sure that it's manufactured to the highest standards and will give you an excellent ride.

With the change in style of boards has come a change in style of riding too. Where the

you buy you can be sure that its construction and performance will be every bit as good as your kite, giving you the perfect combination to help you get into your new sport.

Speaking of which...

One final word about your equipment choice. Don't be suckered into buying equipment – board or kite – that's beyond your skill level, you'll just have a hard time and risk killing your interest off for life. Going to a Kiteboarding School will give you a chance to test different equipment before you buy. When the time comes, be honest about your level and buy accordingly. If you look after it well and learn quickly you can always trade up your beginner gear later, or keep it to lend a friend to help them get started. Speaking of which…

big volume directionals are great for planing and wave riding, small twin tips and wakeboards are ridden much more aggressively on the edges and used for spectacular jumps. Competition riding, which is the inspiration for so much of the media coverage and public interest, exists in four main formats, at least on the major tours and event circuit.

Freestyle : free riding with the emphasis on tricks and fluid riding, aerial gymnastics, transitions and variety of moves, includes rota-

▲ Perfect cruising conditions, light chop and a smooth wind

tions, grabs, board-off moves, handle passes etc. Hang Time: simply explained, who can stay up in the air longest (not necessarily the biggest jump). Wave Riding: a more surf style of riding aiming to exploit the wave's contours to execute moves such as off-the-lips and bottoms and getting in the famous 'tube'. KiteSpeed: again self-explanatory, fastest rider over a measured distance, trying to beat windsurfers and sailors to be the first sail-powered entity to break the 50 knot barrier. While the pro riders may well be riding custom boards, the production replicas are very high quality and whatever board

KITEBOARDING

Learn properly from an accredited school or teacher

"Not only is learning at a school safer, you might as well beat up someone else's kit while you're learning! Seriously though, some things are only obvious once you've been told. Little tips learnt alone the hard way are yours in minutes. Learning in a school will give you confidence; you know you're doing it right."

Andreya Wharry, Extreme Academy kiteboarding instructor

Kiteboarding is a serious, extreme sport and has the potential to be highly dangerous. First there's the immense power of the kite, second you're going to be doing this on and sometimes above water, and third the board itself is hard and thin with the potential to injure you. In circumstances such as those (and despite great books like this one), as a complete beginner, much the best thing you can do is go and take a series of lessons at an accredited school. That way, you get the right sort of advice and training in a secure environment with rescue boats, full insurance and all the other creature comforts that make learning easier. You can test out equipment before you buy (assuming you haven't already) and see if you actually think you've got the endurance to get through the learning phase. Everybody says that as a complete beginner you've got to expect to drink a lot of water during your first few sessions. But everybody also says that the fun comes quickly and there's nothing like the experience of your first successful getting up on a kiteboard.

Whether you've come from a boarding background or a kiting background, lessons will still be a good idea as there's at least 50% of the package you know little or nothing about at this stage. Even if you've got board and kite experience, putting the two together is something you will learn faster with proper instruction rather than guesswork.

Accredited by who exactly? The sport itself has developed incredibly quickly from creation in about 1997 / 8 to next big thing by 2005, and a lot of its growth and history has been pretty anarchic. Some countries have a national body overseeing their sport, how that functions varies enormously depending on which country you're in. In Britain, kiteboarding competitions and school accreditation, safety guidelines and insurance etc. are provided by a volunteer body, the BKSA. (British KiteSurf Association). The BKSA has a permanent office address but most contact is made via their website and by email. Just over the channel in France it falls under the jurisdiction of a long-standing professional body overseeing all wind sports, the F.F.V.L., able to offer technical, financial and logistical support to the developing sport, as well as contact with sponsors and government. Seems we Brits always take a bit longer to recognise a good thing when we see one ! Professional or amateur, membership of an organisation such as the BKSA costs relatively little (compared to the equipment) and, importantly, usually includes 3rd party liability insurance, making it an even better investment. You will usually find classes available via your local kite or windsurf dealer, at a wind or watersports centre, marina, beach windsurf school…

There's also a worldwide body which has a similar function, instructs instructors, approves courses and issues test 'standards' for equipment. It's called the IKO, the International Kiteboarding Organisation. The IKO is sponsored by a number of big name manufacturers as a means of safely bringing newcomers in and promoting and co-ordinating the safe development of the sport. Check that your school is either BKSA or IKO accredited before you book.

A good kiteboard school will have classes for different skill levels of rider. Be honest about your skill level when choosing your course. Courses are structured to deal with your skill level and progression and, like all sports, you need to fully master the basics first and foremost. A typical beginner course will take you all the way from beach flying with small kites, through body dragging in the shallows, to getting up on the board. And check out the site too if possible in advance. The best possible conditions for learning are somewhere with plenty of space, flat water and smooth wind but also water that is shallow over a large area. During the learning phase you're going to spend a lot of time falling in the water and re-starting. Somewhere with good shallow 'lagoon' water will make the process of getting back in position to re-start much, much easier and save you a lot of drinking time, in both senses.

STARTING UP AND GETTING UPWIND

"If you're looking for a completely different kind of buzz from your sport it's got to be kiteboarding; it's not that hard to learn and you will find it exciting on the very first day".

Peter Trow, Flexifoil International team kiteboarder

Whichever way you learn there's going to come a point at which you're ready to make your first attempts to get up on the board. For some people it will all 'click' very quickly, for others it may take longer and more attempts. But don't despair, within a day or so you should be able to go a short distance in both directions and start getting your first big kiteboarding sensations.

Once you've got your kite launched there are two distinct stages to starting up. The first is getting yourself attached to the board, then taking kite and board to the water. The second stage is actually getting up and riding on the board. If you're a beginner rider you'll be best off using a large-volume twin tip. You're going to need good conditions to help you learn. In kiteboarding terms that means anything from about 8 knots of wind speed up as far as 15 using a 12 or 10 m2

kite. Anything more than that and things can start to happen a bit too fast and hard. Anything less and you'll have so little power you won't get up on the board. Another factor you must consider is wind direction. Offshore wind is to be avoided at all costs. Apart from being very lumpy and gusty, making everything difficult, it will blow you out to the open sea and maximum danger. Respect the elements to the max and they won't mistreat you. An onshore wind, while almost certainly smooth, will have the tendency to blow you onto the beach as you inevitably travel more downwind at first, that's if you can even make out past the beach/shore break of waves at all.

The best winds are side-shore, blowing along the beach, or cross-on, blowing diagonally onto the beach. These two allow you to go downwind without getting too far from land

and, if you're able to successfully tack or reach across the wind, to run out from the beach and back in to your start point again, better still, get back upwind beyond your start point. Once you can get back upwind that means you can afford to start trying some downwind runs, or some jumps, knowing that you can regain all the distance lost. The better your skill level and the more competent and confident you are, the further you'll be able to go from your start point. You should never, however under any circumstances, ride out of sight of land. That shouldn't be a factor if you're riding on a lagoon or lake, where you'll also have the advantage of being able to make your first runs downwind safe in the knowledge that you'll soon be arriving at the other side.

When you're sure that conditions are good and you've made all your preparations:

- Launch the kite on the edge of the wind window and steer it carefully up to the zenith.

- If you fly hooked into the de-power loop you can activate it or the quick release if you get into difficulties. At this point you should be able to control the kite with one hand near the centre of the bar, keeping it stable in the minimum power position at the zenith.

- Having established total control over the kite, it's time to attend to the other half of the equation, the board. Locate your board and, keeping one hand and one

◀ Leaning back and edging hard against the pull is a fantastic feeling eye on the kite, attach your board leash to your ankle with your free hand.

■ Keeping the kite at the zenith, pick up the board with your free hand, either by the grab handle or tucked under your arm, and make your way carefully to the water – move the kite slightly over towards the water and it will pull you there – walking far enough out for you and the board to be able to float, preferably to between knee and thigh depth.

If your kite skills are good enough you'll be able to get in and out of the water with ease. Practise that sequence until you're completely comfortable with the whole process. What comes next is more difficult in the sense that now you'll be multi-functioning, kite and board together. Be confident, go for it, you'll be amazed how easy it was once you've got it. To prepare for your water start, position the board in front/downwind of you. Try going to your 'good' side first (everyone has a good and bad side to begin with). It's easier to move the board than yourself so bring the board in front of you so that you're facing it. Hold the board by its grab handle or by the rear strap, and it will be easier to manoeuvre.

■ Position the board so it's pointing across and slightly down wind and tilt it at an angle so that you can easily get your feet into the straps. Start with your front/lead foot, then the rear. Try to get your feet in as quickly as possible, this is the most awkward phase,

▶ Waterstart, getting up and moving on a kiteboard
(top left to bottom right)

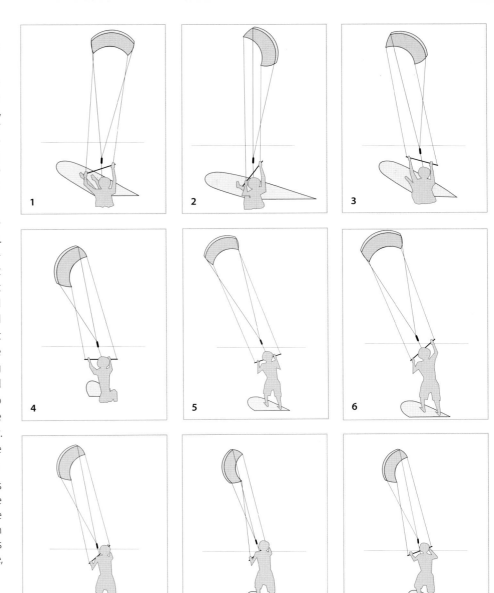

you will end up sitting or lying on your back in the water staring up at your kite. As you put your front foot in, if the kite starts to power up again pull slightly with your front hand and press the board with your front foot a little to adjust your position.

- Steer the kite carefully slightly back across the top of the wind window, to the 'rear' window, opposite from the direction you want to go in. Careful not to let it go too far behind or too low.

- Now, steer the kite back across the wind window towards the side you want to move towards, diving the kite down into the window at 45 degrees as you do so to power it up. Pulling the control bar towards you will help increase the power if necessary. Be careful not to bring the kite too low or it will pull you forwards before you're ready. Keep your knees bent and lean back slightly to lever against the power.

- As you feel yourself being pulled forwards, brace your legs using your heels to 'wedge' the flat of the board against the water, straightening your front leg if possible. Steer the kite up the wind window, working the 'S' pattern to get yourself up and moving. Remember, you may need to sheet out with the control bar to help the kite climb. Keep your legs braced and let the kite pull you gradually up on the board as it climbs the wind window. Strong or light wind, once you're moving steadily forwards slightly downwind, you will need to press with your rear heel to dig the rear edge in to aim the board more upwind. Then press more with the toes of your front foot once up and planing to hold your course.

- If the wind's good enough you can 'lock' the kite in position on the edge of the wind window. In any event, once you're moving steadily forwards and edging slightly, apparent wind will start to apply, boosting the kite's power and increasing your speed. Keep your body flexed and work the board with your feet. It's all in the feet at this stage, a balance of rear foot pressure to work the edge, front foot for course holding. Try not to take too much of the kite pull on your arms, let it pull you through the harness on your body and legs, which keeps your centre of gravity lower, use your arms for steering the kite.

Try to relax as much as possible; with the harness on you won't need too much physical strength to control the kite, and too much foot pressure on the board will result in over-steering. Feel the kite pulling you from the waist, your arms are just there to control the steering. If all goes according to plan you'll be up on your board and planing, skimming across the surface of the water with the upwind edge of the board carving into the water to work against the kite's pull. It may take a few attempts to actually get up. And it will take even more to get anywhere near upwind. Your first runs will, unless you're one of those amazingly gifted people who can do anything first time, take you downwind. Stick at it, a relatively small amount of time invested now will pay off very quickly.

There are a couple of things to avoid that will make learning the water start easier: too big a kite size/too much power on your first few attempts, if you haven't yet got used to big power you'll never get up; bringing the kite too low or too far into the wind window which will give too much lateral pull and heave you forwards, straight off your board. Using a smaller kite means that you'll have to learn to 'work' the kite more than might be the case later, when you've mastered getting up and can afford to try with more power.

Learning the water start is, for obvious reasons, fundamental to all your future activity. You will need to use this technique whenever you fall in the water, once you've re-launched your kite if that has ended up in the water too. Practise water starting to both sides, good and bad, so that you're comfortable getting up and planing in either direction.

There's an alternative to the water start, one you can use closer to dry land, or may have to deploy if the water you're riding simply isn't deep enough for a water start. Not surprisingly it's known as the beach start. It's trickier to get right because it all happens quicker but it's a much cooler, 'cleaner' departure. For this one you need knee depth water at most and to have your board, as before, in front of you, pointing across and slightly downwind. You should be hooked onto your harness on the chicken loop.

- Park your kite up at the zenith and put your front foot in its strap. Careful at this point, the one-foot board-hop could happen if you make a wrong move with the kite.

- Get some power back into your kite by pulling your control bar towards you, closing the trailing edge of the kite, bringing it slowly down the wind window. You will feel the power come on and yourself being gradually lifted.

- As the power in the kite lifts you up, pull on one side of your control bar to dive it down and swing it over towards the side of the wind window you want to move towards. At the same time, step up onto the board with your rear foot, placing it as close to the strap as you can get it (in if possible) so you can stabilise quickly.

- Keep the kite powered-up and moving towards the edge of the wind window to gain apparent wind and even more power.

- Once you're moving forward, stable and powered-up, you can get your rear foot properly into its strap, adjust your body position and dig the back edge in to work the board back up wind.

- With both feet in their straps you can concentrate on planing and keeping the kite well powered-up. It's all in the feet again.

If the wind is strong enough, with a four line kite you can virtually 'lock' it in position at 45 degrees to the water and concentrate on steering, holding your line across wind by working the back edge of the board. That apparent wind factor means the more you can steer the board across and slightly upwind the faster you will be able to go. If you want

▶ Riding toeside means leaning forward rather than back

so they can get out and go bonkers, massively powered up on their tiny trick boards. Ironically there are even people who've succeeded in 'stacking' two LEI kites together, giving a total sail area of over 25 m2, and being able to get upwind in as little as 5 knots because of it. Old habits die hard it seems, I wouldn't mind betting the person who thought of that started off their power kiting career flying a stack of Flexifoil power kites.

CHANGING DIRECTION AND TURNING ROUND

"The skills you learn from old-school directionals benefit wave and frontside riding later. Even on flat water it's really good fun doing a hard carve jibe on a twin tip or wakeboard and popping the board back round on the exit."

Andreya Wharry, Flexifoil team kiteboarder, Extreme Academy kiteboard instructor

For those of you aren't familiar with the subject, we're talking about that old windsurfing stumbling block, jibing. That means turning your board round to go back the way you came. Thankfully for beginners, it's almost obsolete now, but there was a time when jibing was a fundamental part of the whole package. Nowadays it's possible to learn kiteboarding on a twin tip board, so technically speaking, goodbye jibe.

Jibing a traditional directional board is actually quite complicated, as any wizened

to try and get further upwind, with the water to lever against you can bring the kite further down the wind window to power up, at the same time using heel pressure to carve the edge into the water, wedging the board and pointing it more upwind. Once you're pointing the right way take the kite slightly back up the edge of the window and press with the front foot on the board to straighten up again.

If the wind is on the light side for your size of kite, you will need to 'work' it more using the 'S' pattern. The effect of this on the board is that as the kite descends towards the bot-

▲ Adjustable, ergonomic foot straps and super-grippy pads are standard on most kiteboards

tom of the S it picks up power, accelerating towards the bottom edge of the window. That's when you use your rear heel to steer upwind. The kite will gradually lose power as it climbs back towards the top of its S before the cycle begins again so you may need more front foot toe pressure to help the board plane. You need to find a good rhythm of powering up, increasing speed, turning upwind and then gradually straightening again as the kite climbs. The weaker the wind the more exaggerated the 'S' of the kite and weave pattern of the board.

Of course you could use a big 'floaty' board in light wind but riders are generally happier waiting on the beach for the wind to build up

▲ Wave riding has taken kiteboarding back to its surf roots

old windsurfer will tell you. That was one of the reasons Twin Tips were created, first to eliminate the tricky stage of jibing as a hindrance to progress (lesson learned from windsurfing), second to facilitate an altogether 'trickier' (as in range and variety of tricks) style of riding for people who pro-

gressed beyond the basic level. But you still need to know how to go back the way you came. In fact we described almost the identical sequence in the kite landboard chapter earlier in the book, those being twin tips too. It's a logical process of manoeuvres with the kite and board, the object being over time to learn to change/reverse direction without coming to a complete stop, keeping

yourself powered up and moving. One step at a time however…

■ As you're planing along, steer the kite slowly up the edge to top centre window, pushing your bar away so it will lose power and you will slow down. Edging a little will help you 'brake'.

■ As you slow down almost to a stop, shift your weight towards the centre of the

143

board, more upright body position, ready to go back the other way.

- Before you feel the board stop completely and start to sink, steer the kite towards the edge you want to move towards, diving it down in the window and bracing your body for the power coming back on, leading with the other foot. If the board does wallow at this point you will need to water start to get back up again.

- Lock your kite in position, lean back, find your balance and foot pressure points and away you go leading with your other foot.

If you can start up, plane on the board, work the edges to go upwind a bit more and turn round to get back to your start point you've got all the basic manoeuvres you need to start out in the exciting world of kiteboarding, the most exhilarating and fastest-growing extreme sport around. Now it's practise, practise, practise. You will learn a lot faster at this stage by riding with other, more experienced riders, watching what they do, asking them how they do it. With your own growing level of skill and experience and the benefit of theirs you will progress quicker and soon be ready for some more radical and dangerous moves.

But before we move on, lets look at a twin tip jibe alternative that is in fact an advanced manoeuvre, one you'll be able to start learning once you've got

the basics mastered. It will mean you learning to ride on the opposite edge, the toe/frontside edge and flying the kite over your lead shoulder, learning a new set of balance and pressure points on the board. It's an advanced move so don't be disappointed if you don't get it straight away, keep on practicing and it will come.

The problem with the old directional jibe was the complicated foot movements out of the straps to get across to the other side of the board for the return run.

No tricky foot movements are needed on your twin tip, making it in principle faster and easier, but with the added technicality of a big shift of body weight and body position, coming out of the turn leaning forwards as opposed to the more natural backwards lean, a toeside/frontside carve turn.

- As you're riding along, try to shift your weight so the board is flat rather than riding on the edge, use front foot / toe pressure which will also begin to initiate the turn. At the same time start moving your kite up the wind window towards the zenith without letting it get too far over and pulling you off. Sheet out a little to reduce pull and help the kite climb quickly.

- Now you need to really commit to the turn by pressing more with your front foot toes to bring the board flat then over to its toeside edge, body position more upright.

◄ Kite high, board pointing upwind, now you can step out of the straps

As you increase the toeside pressure, carving the board through it's turn, shift your weight forwards more. The toe side pressure will turn the board more quickly. At the same time you'll need something to lean against so you need to swing the kite over hard to the other side of the window (to your new direction of travel), sheet in to power up, diving it down for more power if necessary.

You can use the kite's lift/power to simply 'pop' the board back round to ride normally again at almost any point after the jibe. With plenty of power in the kite you quickly lift both feet and pivot your legs, angling the board correctly (heelside down) to land planing smoothly.

The things to avoid if you want to have the best chance of hitting a good toeside carve are: not having enough forward speed going into the manoeuvre; not tilting the board enough; allowing too much power back into your kite too soon resulting in wipe out; not getting your kite going soon enough to power up again resulting in sinking. It's a lot to think about and again may take you many attempts to get right. The key is in timing everything right to make it one continuous and smooth movement, turning the board and getting it moving again quickly.

STOPPING

Hopefully you're only going to need to stop for one reason, when you want to get back onto dry land for a break. But other emergencies might well dictate that you need to be able to stop dead out on the water. To stop fast you need to be travelling fast and with power. Since you'll be learning 'under-powered' your stop will be more gradual. A dead stop will sink you for sure. Even on a larger volume directional board you will find yourself down in the water, although your kite should be safely positioned and you shouldn't need to water launch it.

- As you are reaching across the wind (and are nearing the beach), start steering the kite up the edge of the wind window to lose power and slow down. Push the control bar slightly away from you to open the trailing edge of the kite and de-power.

- At the same time start leaning back to work the rear edge and turn your board upwind.

- Steer the kite to the zenith with minimum power, being careful not to let it fall forwards, and when the board is pointing upwind press with your front foot to bring the board and yourself upright.

- Step out of the straps and off the board quickly and, keeping the kite stable at the zenith with one hand (keep some pressure on the rear lines to prevent the kite over-flying), pick up your board with the other and leave the water. Finally detach yourself from the board and follow the normal procedure for landing.

The idea is to stop close enough to dry land to be in shallow water and step off the board in your depth, staying on your feet. If you have to execute your stop as an emergency stop (or in deeper water) obviously you won't have that luxury. If you always maintain a good downwind safety margin, perhaps you won't need to use it but there's a simple, effective and fairly crude way of emergency stopping, one that won't take much practice to master.

- As you're riding along and you perceive a need to stop fast, first of all push hard downwards with your rear foot. This stalls the board, turning it hard upwind.

- As the board stalls, sit down hard (arse first) in the water. The action of these two manoeuvres will automatically take your kite to the edge of the window, as long as you keep even pressure on the lines.

- From there you can manoeuvre the kite steadily back up the edge of the wind window to the zenith.

With your kite stable up at the zenith, it will be another chance to practise your water re-start. It's all a question of timing as usual. With skill and practice you'll be riding more powered up and able to stop suddenly, but always be careful not to get the kite either too far behind you (or it will pull you over) or too powered up (in which case you'll be heading for an unexpected jump). Stopping at exactly the right place near the beach is an acquired skill. Whatever type of board you're on, don't approach your landing spot with too much speed, always err on the side of caution.

JUMPING

"For maximum adrenaline unhook, edge hard, send your kite and boost off your edge. Then you'll know what it's like to be a stone in a catapult."

Richard Boudia, Flexifoil International team kiteboarder

It's one thing checking out the great photos in kiteboarding magazines and books such as this, the very latest competition moves on the latest videos and DVDs, but it's quite another actually witnessing a skilful rider (better still in a big competition) hitting some big airs. As soon as you see it you know you want to give it a go. It's sick, it's cool, it's totally impressive and the hang time is amazing. With power control a rider can even turn the power level up while in the air to extend a jump. With tricks besides. Watching the likes of Aaron Hadlow, Richard Boudia, Caroline Freitas and Co. flying past, 10 metres above the water, upside down, with their board in their hands is a huge attention grabber and is one of the main reasons so many people want to learn the sport.

Richard Boudia's advice about jumping unhooked applies to more advanced jumps such as the Handle Pass or Kiteloop. Before the invention of de-power systems and quick releases, riding hooked in to the one, fixed

◀ Complex aerial gymnastics score heavily at freestyle contests

harness loop on your control bar meant always having maximum pull. Riders generally jumped unhooked for safety reasons, so they could let go of the kite in case of a crash. Nowadays that's not necessary, you'll be safer riding through the chicken loop. There are three distinct phases to each jump: preparation and getting airborne; in the air ; the landing. It may take longer to learn the final element and you must be prepared once again for a few falls and some water drinking, having just learned how to ride well enough not to. No gain without pain. Try small jumps at first until you've mastered the mechanics. Then you can start going for bigger, better, more complicated jumps. And that generally means bigger wipe-outs. At least as a kiteboarder you've got the cushioning water to land in rather than a hard surface to slam into. Nevertheless, be careful, that water can still seem hard as concrete and hurt a great deal if you hit it at speed. Thought about an impact vest?

For your first attempts it will be better if you're on flat water rather than waves or a swell. Learn how to jump properly first, you can start playing trampolines with the water contours later on. As ever you want a smooth wind, strong enough to get you off the water but not so much that everything happens too fast or too hard. Try with a medium size kite while you get used to the mechanics, technique and sensations. Remember, this is pretty much maxi danger : in the air, over water, powered by a big kite and not necessarily in 100% control of what

happens next, however good you are. That's why it's better to be hooked onto the chicken loop. It allows you to control the power before and during the jump and makes it simple to let go of everything if you get into difficulties in mid jump.

Jumping almost always moves you some distance downwind during the time that you're in the air, bigger the jump, greater the downwind travel. Be ready for this, make sure you've got a clear zone at least three kite line lengths downwind before you start your attempts. That means clear of other riders / water users but also rocks, moored boats, the beach itself, piers, jetties, anything that can pose a potential risk. For a cool jump you need a combination of board speed and good timing. You also need to keep your hands close to the centre of the control bar to avoid over-steering the kite.

- Steer the kite low down (30 degrees) on the edge of the wind window so that you're as powered-up as possible and sailing slightly upwind, pressing hard with your heels to work the edge in the water and sheeting in with your bar. Don't over-edge or you'll stall the kite. You need a good body position to get ready to go air born, knees bent, body flexed and braced, ready to spring.

- Keep working the edge so as not to lose any speed. Start steering the kite so that it comes slightly back into and up the wind window, pulling very slightly with the side of the bar attached to the top wing tip. Keep plenty of tension on the rear lines to power up.

- As you do this try to release some of the pressure on the board so you are less on the edge and more on the flat of the board, moving slightly towards the kite. Keep moving the kite towards centre top of the wind window, pointing straight up, sheeting out slightly to let the kite climb (your body will naturally be extending into the jump position anyway).

- As you release with the board the pull of the kite in centre window is too much to hold. Now, spring into the air letting the kite pull you off the water as you do so. Keep the kite still with a little front hand pressure.

- All being well, you are now airborne and will really feel the lift effect of the kite. Enjoy every split second but keep a careful eye on your kite and make sure is stays where you put it, keep it as directly above your head as possible. For a good landing you'll need to 'send' the kite back into the window at the right moment, just enough to have power for the landing.

- As you feel the jump 'peaking' get back into a good braced, flexed body shape for the landing, which is coming up quickly. Pull with your forward hand to start bringing the kite forwards in the window to land you travelling in the same direction as before you took off. Have a look to make sure it has started turning. Getting the right amount of power back in the kite at the right moment means a softer landing, too much means a hard fast landing.

◀Triple world champion Aaron Hadlow shows off his new board

■ Brace yourself for splashdown. Watch the water as you approach to really spot that landing and if you think you're going too fast with the kite pulling more than you'd like, try and place the board so it's pointing slightly downwind to lose a bit of speed, rear tip slightly before the front to avoid diving the nose of the board into the water. If the opposite happens and you land heavily with little power, dig your rear edge in, steer the board as upwind as possible to try and power the kite up quickly by sheeting in, bringing it low in the window then powering upwards to lift yourself up and get moving again. Bend your knees on landing to absorb any impact and get yourself planing again quickly.

The trick with learning to jump is having the correct kite size up : too big means it will overpower you at the wrong moment and you won't be able to manoeuvre it quickly enough ; too small and it may be too responsive and have insufficient power to maintain speed or give you lift. When you get it right and you start nailing the whole jump you really are on the way to max-ing your kiteboard sensations. Apart from the size of the kite you're flying, the way you manage to set up your jump with the correct timing of board and kite movements dictates how well you'll jump. The harder you can edge without losing speed and the more 'pop' you can get into the moment of initiating the jump, the higher you'll go. Better technique with the same kite and board will often achieve more than

changing up a kite size. And if it's that good to watch, imagine what it must feel like up there on the board.

WATER RE-LAUNCH

"Water re-launching is no fun but with Flexifoil's medium aspect kites it's much easier today than it was 2 or 3 years ago. Easier still if you use a 5th line. Of course the best thing would be to not put your kite in the water in the first place..."

Kirsty Jones, Flexifoil International
team kiteboarder

At every stage of your kiteboarding apprenticeship there's a chance you're going to end up with your kite down in the water. So it's imperative that you know how to water re-launch, to get you and your kite up again. In fact kiteboarders rarely go more than a few hundred metres offshore so if push came to shove, you really couldn't get re-launched and there's no safety boat nearby, you could swim back in with all your equipment. It's very tiring but since you'll have to dry out your kite before you start again you'll have a bit of recovery time once you're back on dry land.

There's a frequently voiced argument that using an inflatable kite makes you lazy and doesn't place enough emphasis on learning to keep it in the air even during crashes. Certainly the idea is that once you progress

beyond learner status the water re-launch shouldn't be needed anywhere near as much. But neither should the technique be so intimidatingly difficult that it's discouraging for learners.

Whichever type of kite you're flying when you end up in the water, it may be as a result of a big wipe out during which you've let go of your kite and come off your board so the first stage is to recover your equipment. If it was a big wipe out you might well be winded and need a few seconds to get your breath and bearings back. It could be hard work to re-launch, especially if there are waves and you're out of your depth in the water. The kite may have landed in any kind of position although the most common is leading edge down, face towards you. It may be in a complete heap because you activated your safety system. And if your safety system isn't a re-ride system you'll be looking at a swim-in anyway. The first thing to check once you've got your bearings is how it's landed.

Next, recover your control bar. If you were hooked in when you crashed but you let go of the bar, pulling on the centre leader line or 5th line will bring it back to you from its position at the 'stop'. If you weren't hooked in you'll need to recover the control gear using the leash. Make sure the lines are not twisted, nor snagged round your legs or anything else that could affect re-launch. Check where your board is, not too far away if you've got your board leash attached. The

153

kite will normally drift downwind of you on the water. If you're not still hooked onto your de-power loop do so now.

The whole point about inflatable kites is their water re-launch capability. Even so it's certainly no cakewalk and just because you've bought an inflatable doesn't mean it does it all automatically. There's still lots to learn and you've got to get it right and there are still 'dead' positions from which there's no recovery no matter how much you spend on equipment and courses. One piece of equipment that will increase your chances of good water re-launch is a 5th line. With a 5th line the kite always lands on its back and keeps its arched shape making it easy to get it into the right position for re-launch. As soon as you've recovered the control gear and fed the 5th line back through its eyelet the kite will roll onto one tip and make its own way to the edge of the wind window ready to launch.

One factor to consider is the kite's aspect ratio. Some competition standard, high performance inflatable kites are enormously elongated (high aspect ratio) and generally more difficult to re-launch because of it. A good beginner kite would be more rounded (low aspect ratio), making it easier to get onto one wing tip, a crucial phase in the re-launch sequence. Inflatable kites can occasionally re-launch themselves when you're not expecting it so watch out for that first and foremost. If the kite has come down on its leading or trailing edge you must first roll it onto its

back, then one wing tip, then help it find its way to the edge of the wind window to re-launch. Be aware of the kite's position in the wind window. Too much power could give you a problem rolling the kite over so try to get off centre wind by walking / swimming to one side or by pulling on one side of the control bar only at first, to move it towards the edge before you attempt the re-launch. Without a 5th line you must move towards the kite to help it roll onto one tip, fine if you're in your depth but much harder if you're out of it! Without snagging your lines round your legs or board you must swim hard towards the kite so that tension goes off the lines and the kite can roll onto its back. Once on its back you pull on one side of the bar to lift one tip and bring the kite up to stand on the other tip, leading edge facing the edge of the wind window. If the kite is already down on one side/wing tip you're lucky, but you will still need to steer the kite to one edge, the one that the leading edge is facing.

- Pull back on the side of the control bar/ two lines attached to the upper tip and walk or swim in the opposite direction to which you are steering the kite at the same time if necessary. With a 5th line the kite will make its own way to the edge of the window without you moving.

- When the kite nears the edge of the window you can pull harder on the lines attached to the upper tip and keep tension on all four lines to lift it off the water.

- Then steer it carefully up the edge of the wind window to the zenith remembering to push forward with your control bar to help the kite climb.

Once airborne again the kite will feel different to fly, heavier and less responsive. This is because of the water on the sail which will start to dry out once the kite is flying again and normal handling returns. Whichever model of kite you're using, unless you've got a 5th line, water re-launch is a relatively advanced technique so you may not master it straight away. A very good idea is to practise in shallow water near the shore until you're confident. That way you'll be ready when it does happen half a mile offshore and won't be so daunted by the prospect.

With your kite back up at the zenith it's time to get up on your board again using your water start. You've already done the hardest part, recovering your kite, and should be up again quickly from here. On rare occasions you may not be so fortunate, there may really be no safety boat and so the final part of your basic kiteboard training is what to do if it all goes horribly wrong…

BACK TO SHORE

It might happen one day and as usual, there's a simple step-by-step procedure, one that you definitely need to practise in shal-

▶ Kite high and steady, ideal for your first jumps

low water before it happens in choppy sea further out than you care to imagine. In those circumstances, if there's no rescue boat around, it becomes not so much a question of getting started again as saving your life. Your board will be on the end of its leash and will be very useful presently for getting everything back to land. In fact now's the time you might be glad of having a big, floaty directional, which will make the whole paddling in process much easier. For now you need to concentrate on finding your control bar or handles and making sure the flying lines aren't twisted around your legs or the board under the water.

Once you've found the control bar/handles start winding in the flying lines whilst swimming slowly towards your kite. Wind as far as just in front of the kite then leave the bar where it is, it will float with the buoyancy of the leader lines.

At this point there are two options, the short self-rescue or the long pack up and paddle in. Some kites come fitted with 'self-rescue' handles. These are located on the wing tips, in the form of vertical fabric bands. By grabbing both handles and bringing the wing tips together, the kite can be used to 'drag' you and your equipment back to shore, even though it's down on the water. It's a crude way of using the kite's power and you won't be able to steer a course as you would on your board with the kite flying. But it will get you downwind, back to the beach in relatively quick time where you'll be able to re-set your gear and re-launch. Learn how

to do it in shallow water, without the lines attached if you like, before you need to use the self-rescue feature for real away from dry land.

The longer option involves deflating the kite and paddling back in and for this you'll be glad if you're wearing extra buoyancy as it can take a while…

- First straighten out the kite. The first thing to do is deflate the vertical battens using the valves, starting with the tips and working your way inwards to the centre one last. Then deflate the leading edge. Each time you deflate a tube, try hard not to allow any water in and once they're deflated close the valves properly.

- Place the control bar on one tip and roll the kite up around the control bar.

- With the kite rolled you can put it on your board. Take your harness off so the hook doesn't cause discomfort while lying on the board, and use it to attach the rolled kite to your board, or attach it to the rear strap. If you've got a big volume board with plenty of buoyancy you can now lie on the kite and board and paddle back in. Otherwise, if you're on a small board that won't support your weight, tow the board, kite and harness behind you on the board leash as you swim your way back in.

Once you're back to dry land it's time to re-inflate those tubes and check that the flying lines are ok before getting yourself re-launched and re-started. You can practice all this on those days when there's enough

wind to fly the kite but not to get up on the board. Make sure it's second nature to you before the issue is forced on you in less forgiving circumstances.

BASIC RULES FOR KITEBOARDING SAFETY

When you start playing around with the awesome power of big traction kites and then add the extra risk factor of water it's a recipe for extreme fun but also for extreme danger. Safety first, second and third is very much the order of the day: as has been mentioned, manufacturers have gone to considerable lengths to make the equipment safer every year, now it's up to you to follow suit in your approach to your kiteboarding. Safety was a primary reason for the founding of associations and accrediting organisations all over the world.

Many of the international, national and regional associations quickly took on the role of educating riders and training trainers as soon as the new sport started getting attention and attracting newcomers. They have all been working to a similar set of basic safety guidelines, which apply to riders of all skill levels and which all beginner riders are required to learn. The BKSA (British KiteSurf Association) was one of the earliest to form. They identified a number of basic skills a rider

▶ Water re-launching a four line kite

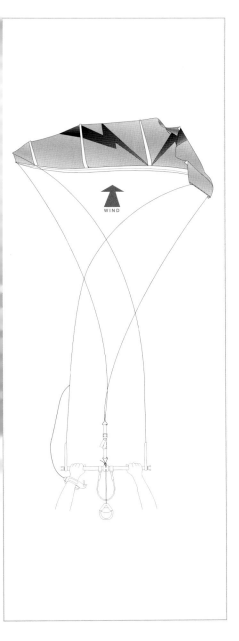

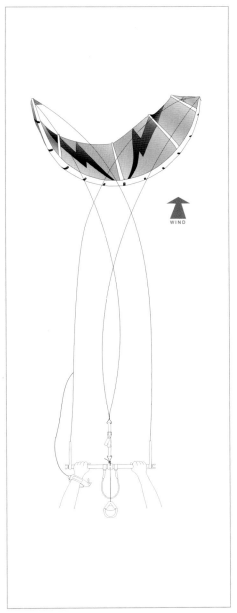

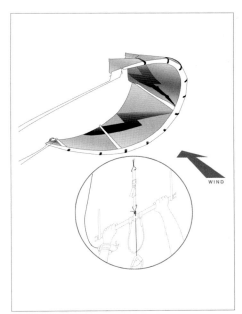

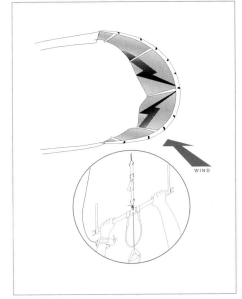

should have acquired in order to move successfully onto the water. With thanks to the BKSA, those guidelines are reprinted here in full.

Kiteboarding is an extreme sport and is therefore potentially dangerous to both the kiteboarder and others. The most important element is rider responsibility, the first level of safety is the rider him/herself.

Code of conduct

Many people use the beaches and water around Britain for a variety of activities. Kitesurfing/kiteboarding can be potentially hazardous unless certain precautions are taken. This is a voluntary code of conduct, but one firmly based in commonsense and co-operation and worth adhering to.

Kiteboarding should not be attempted unless you are a competent swimmer, hold third party insurance and have undergone appropriate (BKSA/IKO) instruction.

The minimum competence levels are considered to be :

Level 1 : Kite Flying Skills

1 Understand all aspects of safe handling of kites on land and water.

2 Able to launch and land (unaided) on a specified spot on land.

Level 2 : Basic Water Skills

1 Body surfing with kite (along and back to shore).

2 Water launching onto board.

Level 3 : Basic Kiteboarding Skills

1 Getting on a board and travelling a distance under kite power.

2 Emergency stop on water – getting off the board quickly and stopping with the kite aloft.

3 Returning to base on land either by kiteboarding, paddling or body surfing.

Kiteboarding Road Rules

■ Be sure that you can handle the prevailing weather conditions and never sail in offshore winds. If in doubt, don't go out.

■ The upwind rider gives way to the downwind rider.

■ The rider on port tack gives way to the rider on starboard tack.

■ Kiteboarders using the seafront should give way to other water users and retreat to a safe zone outside the navigational channel when other craft approach.

■ The seafront can get exceptionally busy both on the beach and on the water. No matter how competent you are, or how good the conditions look, never risk the safety of others.

■ Always maintain a 50 metre downwind safety zone between yourself and other craft. In the event of coming into conflict with other water users stabilize your kite at the top of the window.

■ Never kiteboard within 50 metres of any moored vessel.

■ Never kiteboard in or near to the bathing areas and swimmers, buoys and boat moorings.

■ Never practice jumps on land or close to the beach.

■ When returning to the beach, give way to riders who are launching.

General safety guidelines

■ The BKSA very strongly recommend that a helmet or head protector is worn at all times when kiteboarding.

■ Check the local weather conditions before riding and ensure that you fully understand tidal currents and how they may affect the riding area. The currents along many (British) seafronts can be more like fast flowing rivers and are potentially dangerous.

■ If you lose your kite or board whilst on the water, always notify the rescue services that you are safe so they don't waste time and money mounting a search. It's recommended that you write your name, address, and contact number on all your equipment.

■ Always keep your flying lines away from people, animals and craft on land and water. Do not leave your equipment unattended on the beach. Be polite to other beach users.

■ Always act in a responsible manner. If new or careless riders turn up, talk to them about the risks. Take the time to explain how to get into the sport safely, and where to obtain adequate, professional instruction.

▶ A great spot, plenty of space on the water and on the beac

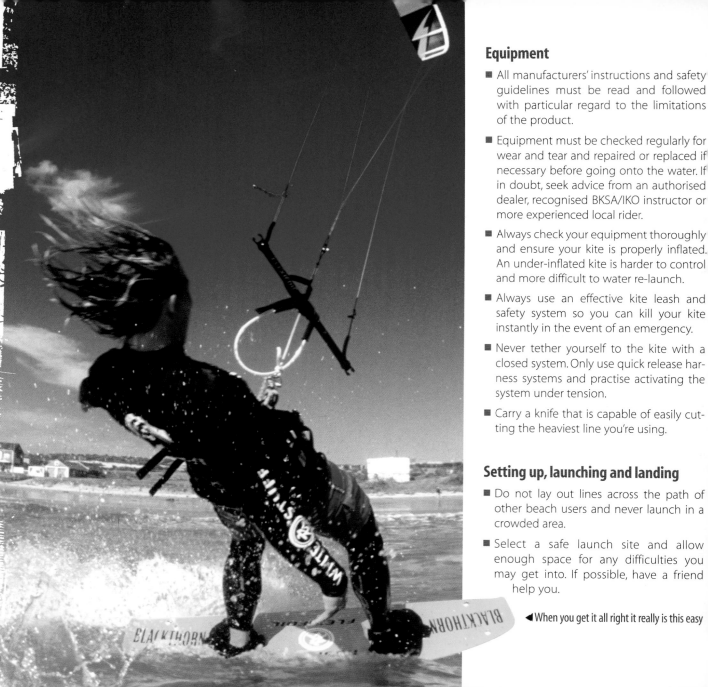

Equipment

- All manufacturers' instructions and safety guidelines must be read and followed with particular regard to the limitations of the product.

- Equipment must be checked regularly for wear and tear and repaired or replaced if necessary before going onto the water. If in doubt, seek advice from an authorised dealer, recognised BKSA/IKO instructor or more experienced local rider.

- Always check your equipment thoroughly and ensure your kite is properly inflated. An under-inflated kite is harder to control and more difficult to water re-launch.

- Always use an effective kite leash and safety system so you can kill your kite instantly in the event of an emergency.

- Never tether yourself to the kite with a closed system. Only use quick release harness systems and practise activating the system under tension.

- Carry a knife that is capable of easily cutting the heaviest line you're using.

Setting up, launching and landing

- Do not lay out lines across the path of other beach users and never launch in a crowded area.

- Select a safe launch site and allow enough space for any difficulties you may get into. If possible, have a friend help you.

◀ When you get it all right it really is this easy

- Never ask an inexperienced member of the public to assist.

- Extra care should be taken when the beach is busy. Occasionally it may be too busy to launch safely without having a designated launch area in operation.

- Prevent kites from re-launching by weighting them with sand and ensure that sand will not be dropped on other beach users when self-launching.

- Fully disable unattended kites and wind lines in up to the kite so as not to inconvenience other beach users.

- Look out for other riders returning to shore and be ready to help them land their kites.

- Never kiteboard in areas congested with swimmers, boats, other craft or obstacles.

- If you kiteboard alone let someone know where you are going and what time you expect to return.

- Always maintain a downwind safety zone especially when jumping. Look before you jump.

- Never ride so far away from shore that you cannot swim back in an emergency.

- All riders should be familiarised with rescue signals and practice self-rescue pack down manoeuvres when undergoing kiteboard training with BKSA/IKO instructors.

- If you need to swim in, kill the power in your kite, wind the lines onto the bar and deflate the leading edge.

OTHER ESSENTIAL EQUIPMENT

The full list of kiteboarding essentials depends to a large extent on where you're going to do the majority of your riding. The air and water temperature will make a huge difference, for example, to the thickness of your wetsuit, and indeed whether you wear one at all. But suffice to say there's an armoury of other pieces of equipment aside from the board and kite that you'll need to have before you can get out on the water, wherever you're planning to plane.

- Harness. Absolutely essential. Generally available in two styles, the belt harness and the seat harness. The former fitting round the waist and the other a full crotch fit. The seat version helps get the centre of pull and balance much lower making boarding more stable, a better option for beginners.

- Wetsuit. Absolutely essential. Available in different thicknesses (anywhere from 3 to 7 mm) depending on how cold it's likely to be, 3 to 5 being the most common. Also in different leg and arm lengths with a shorty suit in 3 mm being the kind of thing for warm water riding. Even in tropical waters, if you plan to ride all day a shorty suit can protect you from crash landings, sunburn and hypothermia. Different men's and women's fits. Always try on in the shop before you buy. If they won't let you, go somewhere else.

- Crash Helmet. Absolutely essential. There's no excuse for not wearing one.

- Impact vest. Great for absorbing high impact crashes. Some now available with integral harness.

- Board Leash. Attaches the board to your ankle or rear of your harness via a Velcro strap fastening and length (2 metres approx.) of vinyl cord. You can ride without one if you like but you're going to be chasing your board all over the place. Watch out for the board recoiling though.

- Wind meter. Expect to pay a lot for any handheld meter with accuracy.

- Puncture repair kit. Absolutely essential. Like a bicycle puncture repair kit but for the inflatable tubes (bladders) that are vital to your kite's functioning.

- Basic human repair kit. Plasters, antiseptic, bandages, sling, this is an extreme sport remember?

- Sun cream/ultra violet protection for those parts of you not covered by your suit and which will be exposed to the elements all day.

- Sunglasses. As above but for your eyes.

That's what you need to get you going. What about all those things that can happen during the day (other than a tube bursting) that you need to cover yourself for ? The more you kiteboard the more gear you're going to accumulate for doing different things and the more potential for hardware failure to spoil your day out.

- Spare flying line sets in case of a damaged or broken line.
- Spare control bar.
- Splicing and sleeving kit for making adjustments/repairs to flying lines.
- Spare fins for your board.
- Spare straps/bindings.
- Tool kit with spare fittings for fins and bindings.
- Spare harness (an old one perhaps).
- Different types of board depending on the conditions, a larger volume directional or twin tip for light winds and a wake or mini board for strong winds and flat water.
- A reserve supply of energy bars and / or drinks in case, as can easily happen, you stay out riding a long time and need to get emergency energy in your body once you're back on dry land. And remember to take plenty of fresh water to drink.
- A waterproof watch so you can actually keep track of time instead of losing it.

Kiteboarding's not an easy sport if you haven't got your own wheels or access to someone else's, as you'll have gathered. Unless you belong to a club or are on holiday somewhere where you can rent equipment. Likewise, if you decide you want to start exploring some of the more exotic spots around the world, unless you're very clever you're going to end up with hefty excess baggage charges from the airlines. And don't forget, you'll need somewhere to store it all as well, maybe it's time to start looking in the estate agents' for that bigger house, one nearer the sea for instance…

◄Riding the winds of change: kiteboarding is now established worldwide

CARE OF THE KITE

7

CARE OF YOUR KITE AND KIT

The more power kiting that you do the more equipment you're going to accumulate and the more serious and potentially dangerous its purpose often becomes. The object is to enjoy the danger whilst minimising the risk, both to yourself and others. And then there are the kites and flying lines that control them. It can all potentially either endanger or save your life (or someone else's) and needs to be looked after and maintained accordingly. Apart from anything else, you've quite possibly spent a good deal of your hard-earned money buying them. And who knows, one day you might even want to start selling some of it second hand in which case, the better the condition it's in the more you'll get for it.

Nothing deteriorates ripstop nylon sail cloth and other fabrics quite as efficiently as ultra violet light from the sun. Unless it's salt water. And sand. Or all three together. So, while beach sites are great for wind and space, they're also a potential hazard for your kites. Yes it's a good idea to have different kites ready to use in case of changing wind, but bear in mind that a kite subjected to prolonged exposure to bright sunlight will

◀ Check the leading edge of Flexis for small nicks and tears
▶ Prolonged exposure to UV deteriorates nylon

quickly fade and deteriorate. If your kite gets wet with salt water you should rinse the fabric when you get it home. Warm (not hot), very mildly soapy water in a hand wash, then cold rinse and dry thoroughly before finally packing away. In fact any kite that is packed away wet from sea or rain on the flying site must be completely dried out at home before storing. Be careful too of tar and oil on beach sites as these are very difficult to remove.

Empty sand out from ram air kites as it will damage the fabric and interfere with flying. Check your kites over regularly, specially for signs of strain around the bridle or flying line attachment points and any damage to the bridle itself. Small fabric tears and holes can be mended with clear adhesive repair tape available from your dealer. Bigger tears or holes or other general repairs should be returned to Flexifoil, either directly or through your dealer. Even with regular heavy use, every weekend, a kite should last you two or three years if looked after properly. After that time it may well

be generally used and stretched, specially if used extensively at or above its wind range limit, to an extent that replacement is the only option. It will certainly never fly again 'as new' as the fabric will have lost its coating and become soft and floppy.

On an inflatable kite you should check over your inflatable tubes regularly, both the bladders themselves and the tubes they fit in. Bladder punctures can be easily repaired in a similar way to a bicycle repair. You may need to put the inflated tube under water to identify the leak before effecting a repair. There are detailed step-by-step instructions in the kite manual for repairing a bladder and, importantly, replacing it correctly in its tube afterwards. Check the leading edge for signs of scuffing or small nicks and tears and the line attachment points to make sure they are secure. And there's a big stress point where the leading edge is joined to the sail. Check along the length of this join.

Pay careful attention to your control lines, leader lines and any stacking lines if flying a stack. Worn leader lines, sleeving or connection loops must be replaced immediately. Snapping a line at 20 mph on your landboard or 5 metres off the water on your kiteboard is no joke. Always wind your lines neatly and avoid dragging them across the ground, specially wet sand. Walk towards them when winding in. Check the lines for any nicks or signs of wear. The lines start

◀ Top: Landboards are relatively low maintenance
◀ Bottom: Over-inflation can lead to burst tubes

their life very smooth and slippery but may rough up with extensive use, specially if used a lot on sand. The sand grains can get in between the fibres and cause friction and wearing, interfering with flying and damaging the lines. Lines which have been used near water and sand, or are simply very dirty, can be rinsed, on their winder, under a running tap of cold water, 'teasing' the lines with your fingers to help wash them clean. Hang the lines somewhere to dry, preferably out of direct sunlight, before packing away. A well looked after set of flying lines should last you two or three years, if not longer, although this will reduce when you start adding the extra stress and loadings of buggying or kiteboarding. A set of kiteboarding lines, for instance, should be replaced every year or so.

Harnesses and control bar harness loops are specially vulnerable to wear and tear with the heavy loading they carry. If you're using a harness check it over regularly for signs of wear, specially round the fastenings and the hook. Likewise your control bar and strop / loop. Unexpected harness or control bar loop failure could cause a real problem. And crash helmets, specially any that have actually taken a few direct knocks, should also be regularly replaced as they become ineffective once damaged.

Buggies are made from stainless steel making them virtually maintenance free.

► Check over bearings and downtube, use a teflon lubricant

Nevertheless, if your buggy is muddy or has been in salt water conditions you are well advised to hose it down thoroughly. Inspect the frame for damage or cracks periodically. Don't attempt any repairs yourself, consult your dealer or Flexifoil International. You can clean the seat by hand wash in warm soapy water, rinsing and drying it out thoroughly before packing away. The wheel bearings will wear with use. This is unavoidable. They are made of hi-tensile rather than stainless steel. There are ways of prolonging their life with regular maintenance. Remove the wheel bolts occasionally and clean them.

Wash the wheels down with cold water and dry them, then spray with a Teflon type lubricant (bike chain type). Check the plastic hub for damage or cracks and replace if necessary. The bearings themselves should be replaced when worn which you can tell if they are reluctant to spin freely even when lubricated or have sideways movement. Same goes for the front fork bushes which are made from tough nylon. You should remove them and clean the assembly occasionally, replacing any worn bushes.

Taking proper care of a kite landboard will help prolong its life. Inspect your board and trucks periodically for damage and cracks and replace as necessary. If the board has been in mud or on a salt water beach hose it down thoroughly with fresh water and dry it off before storing. As with a buggy, wheels and bearings will wear with use, make regular maintenance checks and replace affected parts. Clean regularly and lightly apply

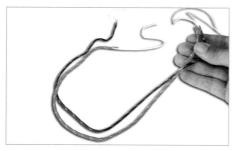

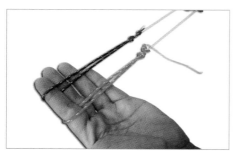

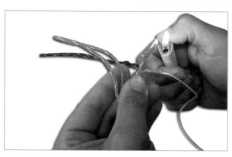

a Teflon based lubricant. Damaged wheel hubs should be replaced immediately, same goes for tyres. Wheel bearings are worn if they don't spin freely or there's lots of sideways movement when they do.

Kiteboards, specially those made from sandwich or other foam construction, are specially vulnerable to the ravages of salt water and must be checked regularly for any knocks, bumps or cracking. Salt water in your board means the board is potentially fatally weakened. Check over your fins and their housings, likewise your bindings and their mountings and around the leash bung wherever that is. Don't take chances, take the board to your local dealer if you have the slightest doubt. They may have a repair workshop on site or will know where to send you or the board.

As a final thought, specially relevant to kiteboarders, it might be worth marking all your kit, with your name and contact details so that if ever you do lose a kite or board out at sea it can be traced back to you and you might have a chance of recovering it.

ADJUSTING YOUR DYNEEMA FLYING LINES

Dyneema flying lines have very little stretch but they do have some and the stretch is not necessarily even. You can generally fly all the stretch out of your lines in a couple of

◀ How to adjust Dyneema flying lines

good sessions at the end of which you may find that one line has stretched more than another. This will cause your kite to fly unevenly and needs to be remedied. Flexifoil line sets now come 'extreme-stretched' to avoid this kind of thing happening. Nevertheless if you do need to re-equalize your lines for any reason, there's a way of doing it that will help use up some time when you're waiting for some wind.

Dyneema flying lines have a length of 'sleeve' roughly 30 cm long at each end to help prevent them breaking with friction where knots are tied. The loop which you use to attach your flying lines to the kite is tied in this sleeved section. To make the adjustment you need to do the following.

■ Peg the loops at the free end of your lines to the ground using your ground stake. Unwind the lines fully and detach the handles or control bar.

■ Pull on all/both lines together to identify which is the longer and by how much. Take the longer line and undo all the knots which form the loop at the unpegged end until the sleeve is free to move along the line. If you've been flying the kite in very strong wind these knots may have pulled very tight so be prepared with your best finger nails, teeth etc. Don't let the end of the Dyneema flying line slip back inside the sleeving, it will be very difficult to get out again.

■ Slide the sleeve along the flying line until it matches the other/s. If you can pull gently on all the lines as you do this it will help make it more accurate. If the sleeve

is difficult to move try holding the end of Dyneema that's poking out and pulling the sleeve from the other end.

■ Re-tie the loop using a single thumb knot at the sleeve end towards the middle of the line to stop it slipping and then another

▲ Wash off sand and salt water after a good session

thumb knot with the sleeved line doubled back on itself to form a good non-slip loop about ten centimetres long. A thumb knot is the most basic form of knot: make a small loop where you want the knot and hold it between finger and thumb ; pass the end of the line round the other side, back through the loop and pull tight.

Flexifoil's latest high performance line sets now have sewn end loops that cannot be adjusted. This is possible because line manufacturers have found a system for fully stretching lines before use, thereby simplifying things and eliminating the need to adjust them.

WHERE TO GO

THE POWER KITE FILES

Where to go?

There are literally thousands of good power kiting spots to visit on the thousands of miles of British coastline, both on and off the beaten track. For pure recreational flying almost any good open site that conforms to all the safety guidelines explained at the beginning of the book will do. For the more serious stuff obviously other criteria, notably the one of having maximum space, and specifically kiteboarding where there is the pre-requirement for water too, snow for snowkiting, will apply.

Once you start getting into serious boarding or buggying you would be much better off heading for one of the recognised sites where you might well find other drivers around. The spot may be covered by insurance and/or have support boats, a building with showers, a shop, a repair shop... If you really want to get out on your own 'on safari', why not join one of the UK's power kite clubs (see next section), which have comprehensive lists of approved sites for kite buggying or boarding for you to choose from and a 'season' of organised events. You can either tag along or go to one of the other sites when they're all at an event somewhere else.

Buggies really need that hard flat sand to run well, kiteboarders in theory have more

◄ Sand, sea and sun, an ideal spot for power kiting

freedom as long as they can find a beach to launch from. Saying that, restrictions do apply and once you start kiteboarding regularly again you should consider joining the BKSA (British Kite Surf Association). Even if you don't join, the BKSA has an excellent web site you can consult that lists literally hundreds of sites all around the UK, with guidance as to where kiteboarding is and isn't practical or encouraged, schools, safety advice and so on. Always check if local restrictions apply. In some cases you need only drive another five minutes to find restriction and hassle free facilities, as was the case in West (restricted) and East (no restrictions) Wittering on the Sussex coast. In many places there are seasonal restrictions linked to holiday periods when the beaches and water are simply too busy to use.

Another source of information is the IKO (International Kiteboarding Organisation). The IKO is an organisation that instructs and co-ordinates the instruction of kiteboard instructors for inflatable kites world-wide. As such it is a great resource of information regarding where to find kiteboarding schools around the world. Contact details for the PKSF, BKSA and IKO are all in the Clubs and Associations section following.

Many dealers and retailers offer individual after sales classes or formally structured courses which you're strongly advised to take up. And wherever you find a dealer you'll find their customers somewhere nearby who will already know the best

places to go. Why not think about a weekend or week long course at one of the power kite centres in the UK ? An intensive course is the best way to learn and it's great fun to go away for the weekend with a group of like-minded people for some intensive amusement and hands-on extreme sport action.

There are dozens of kiteboarding schools to choose from now, many linked to windsurf and other water and extreme sport centres, equipped with rescue craft etc. You'll now find kites in many surf shops with boards and other kiteboarding equipment in many kite shops, both of which, as mentioned, usually offer tuition. Big organisations such as Club Med. and countless smaller companies are offering kiteboarding course holidays in various locations around the world.

It's a bit different for landboarding and buggying. There are fewer recognised centres and schools but probably more informal tuition available. Saying that, there are a number of Flexifoil-approved, dedicated, full-time power kite centres in the UK where you can learn a range of power kiting activities, everything from flying your first Flexifoil to getting up on a kite board and where you can test the full range of Flexifoil equipment. A call to Flexifoil or a visit to **www. flexifoil.com** will quickly tell where the nearest one is to where you are.

If the UK is well blessed with power kiting sites, so too are many other places around the world. Anywhere with good, big, empty

beaches, shallow 'lagoon' water and regular good strength winds. Lots of exotic warm water island locations that are big for wind-surfing are already well established on the kiteboard circuit so you could do worse than start with a trip to Hawaii / Maui, the very nerve centre of all things surf. Closer to home, the Canary Islands offer great winter warmth and excellent wind and beaches and France is the biggest European mar-ket for wind and water sports. But if you really want to go exotic then why not try New Caledonia in the south Pacific, the Madeleine Islands in Canada, Dominican Republic, Martinique or Guadeloupe in the Caribbean, the Greek island of Paros, Tarifa in Spain, Australia, New Zealand, Hood River / The Gorge in America, Copacabana Rio de Janeiro, Madagascar, Egypt, South Africa….. All these destinations have fully equipped and accredited kiteboard schools (more than twenty in Tarifa alone !) and / or a well-established primary location plus good information regarding where else you can explore in the vicinity.

◀ Frequent Flyers Club meetings are best held at the nearest beach
▶ You'll have to travel to find snowkite playgrounds like this

CLUBS, SOCIETIES AND ASSOCIATIONS

There are dozens of groups, clubs and associations you can join, some local, some national and one or two international. And for the 'club' phobic among you let's just remind you of some of the benefits you might find in joining one. Although power kiting in all its forms is growing in popu-larity at a phenomenal rate, individually kiteboarding (all formats combined) and kite buggying are still minority sports and it's helpful to have information resources at your disposal. Joining a group or asso-ciation means access to information of all sorts that can save you learning time and raise your fun levels, help you meet like-minded individuals and find out where are the best places to go. Almost all offer insurance cover, which is a very important consideration, and may well have nego-tiated a bulk discount with favourable rates and very good cover, something you might find much more difficult to match or find at all on your own. For instance, a kiteboarder joining the BKSA gets £5 mil-lion worth of third party liability cover for less than half the price of a control bar as part of their deal.

Having grown in a relatively unplanned, anarchic fashion, power kite sports have had an equally spontaneous approach regarding the development of clubs, soci-eties and associations. Unlike our French friends, where all wind sports are dealt with by the huge, government-funded FFV and FFVL, the UK's clubs are mainly volunteer-run and have tended to develop around popular activities or locations. But be aware that local councils prefer to deal with an organised club or association rather than a rag tag crowd of capable individuals if it ever comes to negotiating access rights etc.

There's been a recent move to combine the individual organising bodies for each sport to form one power kite sports cover-all organisation, which, when all the memberships of all the various regional and national clubs is added together, now has more than 10,000 active members. All being well, that means there will now be somebody looking after your interests at both a practical level (teaching, insurance, event organisation, data bases etc.) and as regards future development, recognition and funding to develop the respective sports nationally and regionally. The PKSF (Power Kite Sports Federation) really do cover everything from flying your first Flexifoil 6' Stacker to hitting those big airs on your AH Pro model board and Fusion kite. The PKSF combines the functions of all the various power kite sports' bodies in the UK, giving them one voice and more clout. A bit like building a big stack out of several individual kites…. They offer combined insurance policies for all types of power kite activities, organise and sanction events, co-ordinate teaching and provide

an important information resource for ALL power kite people. In fact this gives recreational flyers a voice for the first time where previously only the more extreme sports were represented.

Contact for the PKSF can be made direct, or via the existing individual bodies which make up the new group. And all of them will be happy to put you in contact with local groups in your region if that's what you're looking for.

Power Kite Sports Federation (PKSF)

Though still not the finished article, the PKSF already has comprehensive training schemes covering all power kite activities, plus an attractive insurance package. They plan to launch a website during 2006.
Address: PO Box 2893
Dudley
West Midlands DY1 3YT
UK

For Kite Buggy drivers :

British Buggy Club (BBC)

Originally created during the 'first wave' of buggy interest, the BBC caters for all levels of buggy driver and has more recently widened its remit to incorporate any and all power kite sports.

P.O. Box 4015
Smethwick
West Midlands B67 6HJ
UK

Email: admin@britishbuggyclub.co.uk
Web site: www.britishbuggyclub.co.uk

Para Kart Association (PKA)

The buggy club for the competitive-minded. The PKA has affiliated itself with the British Federation of Sand and Land Yacht Clubs who recognise kite buggies as Class 8 Land Yachts for race and insurance purposes. Organises an extensive race series through the year including long distance /time enduros.

Web site: www.pka-online.org.uk

For kiteboarders:

British Kite Surfing Association (BKSA)

The BKSA now has a permanent postal address although the majority of its functions (membership, information, national championships reports etc.) are run through their excellent web site and that is the primary means of contact. They organise national championship competitions and help in the development of training and local groups

and clubs as a means of helping the long-term development of the sport.

Address: PO Box 7871
East Leake
Leicestershire
LE12 6WL

Website: www.kitesurfing.org
Email: info@kitesurfing.org

and for international reference and the whereabouts of approved inflatable kite schools

International Kiteboarding Organisation (IKO)

Web site: www.ikorg.com

General:

Scottish Power Kite Association (SPKA)

Regional association providing a similar function for power kite sports generally in Scotland as the BKSA do for kiteboarding nationally. Excellent web site full of information.

Website: www.spka.co.uk

MAGAZINES, PUBLICATIONS, DVDS AND VIDEOS

There are three English language full colour kiteboarding/power kite magazines published in the UK and plenty more abroad. The vast majority cover kiteboarding pri-

marily or exclusively, but not all. The speed at which all power kite sport markets are growing has made it more feasible to consider publishing a dedicated power kite title. So, let's start with Power Kite Magazine from UK publisher Arcwind, covering all your favourite land based power kite sports – landboarding, buggying, snowkite – bi-monthly, with plenty of reports, features, test reviews, action shots and teaching sequences.

Also from Arcwind, their other specialist kite title, *Kitesurf Magazine*, as the name would imply, a dedicated kiteboarding magazine, focussing heavily on the increasingly active UK scene, but covering some big international events and exotic away trips too. *Kiteworld Magazine* is another

essentially kiteboarding title, this one from UK publisher XCMedia, concentrating more on power kiting around the world. They give some coverage to other land-based power kiting, specially snowkiting, but by far the biggest part of the magazine features kiteboarding, with lots of superb photography from Flexi's favourite snapper, Christian Black. Both titles cover kiteboarding events, tips, advice, board, kite and other equipment tests, plus pages and pages of colour photos from all round the world that will have you really drooling, all blue lagoons, tropical sun and deserted palm-fringed white sand beaches. Just the job to keep your spirits up on those grim, grey, 7mm wetsuit northern hemisphere winter days.

Kiteboarder Magazine is published in America with similar content to the two UK magazines. And try French-published *Stance Mag.* for a (French language) magazine with a free DVD. Many other countries now have their own dedicated kiteboard title or, like Australia, have regular kiteboard supplements available in the established surf / windsurf mags. Depending on your language skills (unless you just like looking at the pictures), just about every European country with a bit of coast now has its own kiteboarding mag. As you can imagine the internet is awash with kiteboard stuff, just type kiteboard/kitesurf/flysurf into your search engine.

As for DVD and video, kiteboarding being such a very visual thing, there are now countless DVDs and videos available crammed full of great action shots, some from competition, others trips, others simply for the hell of it (almost all with the obligatory ha-ha-ha 'wipeouts' section). Check the internet or the kiteboarding magazines for news about new kite DVD / Video releases. There's quite a lot of good quality teaching material too. There are less general power kite DVDs or videos, although you'll find some snowkite and landboard footage on some of the kiteboarding releases. Flexifoil themselves made a famous series of power kiting promo videos in the late 1990s of which the 'Airheads' and 'Power Trip' were the best known. Airheads is still available but Power Trip is now a much sought-after

second hand collectors item only. All in all there are plenty of good vids and DVDs available, far too many to list here but a quick visit to your local kite or surf dealer is sure to be rewarded with a good selection to choose from.

DEALER LIST

If you're reading this and expecting to find a long list of names, addresses and telephone numbers for your nearest stockist then look no further. Because there isn't one. It wouldn't be possible to print them all and it wouldn't be fair to leave any out.

Even just on a UK basis the number of Flexifoil stockists is enormous and, while some of them might not carry all the really serious buggy and boarding equipment, it would be unfair just to list the main dealers. Every one of them, even the little ones and those who only stock a limited range, have helped to make Flexifoil what it is today, one of the biggest names in world wide power kiting circles. Flexifoil's comprehensive distributor and dealer network means that their products are available all over the power kiting world.

There are obvious places to look for Flexifoil products : kite, surf and windsurf shops being the places to start. But you'll also find racks of Flexifoil kites and other accessories in many enlightened extreme sports, outdoor pursuits, roller blade, juggling and toyshops. These in-store displays carry a loop tape power kiting video so you can enjoy some TV thrills and spills while you make your selection. The easiest way to find the nearest appropriate kind of store for you is to contact Flexifoil International direct who will be happy to put you in touch. To save you the embarrassment of a polite 'no' on the phone, Flexifoil do not sell direct to the public at fantastically reduced 'factory' prices, you must use their established dealer network, details from :

Flexifoil International
27 Regal Drive
Soham
Ely
Cambridgeshire CB7 5 BE
Tel: 01353 723131
Fax: 01353 722311
Email: info@flexifoil.co.uk
Website: www.flexifoil.com

INDEX